Diva

COOKING

VICTORIA BLASHFORD-SNELL & JENNIFER JOYCE
PHOTOGRAPHY BY **GEORGIA GLYNN SMITH**

Diva
COOKING

UNASHAMEDLY GLAMOROUS PARTY FOOD

whitecap

DEDICATION
To our boys – Julian, Jack, Patrick, Liam, and Riley

This edition first published in North America in 2002 by Whitecap Books. For more information,
contact Whitecap Books, 351 Lynn Avenue, North Vancouver, British Columbia, Canada V7J 2C4

First published in Great Britain in 2001 by Mitchell Beazley, an imprint of
Octopus Publishing Group Ltd, 2-4 Heron Quays, London E14 4JP

ISBN 1 -55285-371-3

A CIP catalog record for this book is available from the British Library. The authors and publisher will be grateful
for any information that will assist them in keeping future editions up-to-date. Although all reasonable care has
been taken in the preparation of this book, neither the publisher nor the authors can accept liability for any
consequences arising from the use thereof, or from the information contained therein.

Commissioning Editor: Rebecca Spry   Executive Art Editor: Phil Ormerod   Managing Editor: Jamie Grafton
Editors: Susan Fleming and Maggie Pannell   Design: The Senate   Proofreading: Jo Richardson
Production: Alex Wiltshire   Index: John Noble

Typeset in Eurostile

Printed and bound by Toppan Printing Company in China

divacontents

these symbols are used in
the recipe section:

cooking tip

double the quantity

ingredients tip

preparation tip

serving tip

diva**introduction**

We met over the cake counter. It was eight years ago at the infamous Books for Cooks shop on London's Portobello Road. Both of us were working in the tiny kitchen where recipes from hundreds of books are tested on eager customers. Our friendship first revolved around our mutual love of food, but later evolved to encompass the rest of our lives – our children, our husbands, our other interests. Yet all these years later, there is still one thing we focus on most: expanding our culinary skills through the constant, greedy quest for new ingredients, helpful techniques, and useful insights. Yet we are frequently frustrated by the lack of detail in cookbooks and recipes. That's why we decided to write a different kind of book, a book that goes one step further.

In *Diva Cooking* we wanted not only to design delicious dishes, but also to teach you the secrets of preparing ahead, which recipes work well together and how best to handle presentation. That's why all the recipes feature "Diva Dos" and "Diva Don'ts", divulging essential information about how far in advance food can be made, potential pitfalls, doubling quantities, and which colors or fresh herbs to use for garnishing.

To a large extent, creating great dishes is about choosing the right ingredients and understanding how to get the basics right, so we've also included ingredients pages which advise on how to find the highest-quality ingredients and how to cook with them. There are lots of powerful flavors in *Diva Cooking,* too – whether it's sea salt used to enhance tastes or a new chili paste, big tastes always go down well at a party. But knowing how to pair unusual flavors, spices, and herbs isn't always obvious, so *Diva Cooking* features extra ingredients pages on flavors, as well as herbs and spices, to guide you on what they are and how to best use them.

Diva food is party food, and all the recipes in *Diva Cooking* have been created for parties of eight or more. They can all be eaten with a fork while standing up and chatting, but most can also be enjoyed at formal dinner parties. Figuring out a party menu that's balanced in terms of time and complexity can be tricky. You'll find both simple and more complicated dishes in this book, and each recipe has estimated preparation and cooking times; that way, you can match a main dish that takes one hour to prepare with a salad that takes five minutes! No one should be chained to the kitchen for two days preparing for a party.

Diva Cooking doesn't do anything in a small way – we like bold flavors and sizzling style. We love recipes that make a statement: whether through using unusual ingredients, presenting classics beautifully or showcasing big, gutsy tastes. We believe food has to both look great and offer impressive flavor; too often, recipes concentrate on one characteristic at the expense of the other. In this book, however, every recipe guarantees both. That's exactly what *Diva Cooking* is about: cook, eat, and have fun. We do.

divacanapés

avocado & goat cheese crostini with roasted cherry tomatoes

● Makes 20 canapés to serve 10   ● Preparation: 20 minutes   ● Cooking: 40 minutes

This unusual combination of avocado and mild goat cheese works equally well as a crostini topping or dip. It looks beautiful and tastes delicious.

crostini

20 ½-inch-thick slices of day-old French bread, preferably a thin stick

olive oil

roasted cherry tomatoes

10 cherry tomatoes

olive oil

1 tablespoon balsamic vinegar

salt and pepper

avocado purée

1 large ripe avocado, peeled, pitted and chopped

5½ oz fresh, creamy goat cheese

grated zest and juice of ½ lemon

1 tablespoon olive oil

1 garlic clove, peeled

2 shakes of Tabasco sauce

salt and pepper

1 Preheat the oven to 350°F. To make the crostini, place the bread slices on a baking sheet brushed with olive oil. Brush the bread with olive oil. Bake until crispy and golden brown, about 10 minutes. Set aside in a dry place until needed.

2 To roast the cherry tomatoes, preheat the oven to 300°F. Cut the tomatoes in half and place on a baking sheet. Drizzle with olive oil and balsamic vinegar, sprinkle with salt and pepper, and roast for 30 minutes.

3 To make the avocado purée, place all the ingredients in a food processor or blender and purée until smooth. Adjust seasoning to taste.

4 To assemble, place a teaspoon of the avocado purée on top of each crostini, and garnish with a roasted cherry tomato half.

divados

Buy the avocados ahead of time to ensure they are ripe. Vine-ripened tomatoes can be used instead of roasted cherry tomatoes. Choose the thinnest French bread available.

You can make the crostini a week ahead and store in an airtight container. The avocado purée can be made one day ahead. Cover, with plastic wrap touching the purée to remove all air, then chill.

Flat-leaf (Italian) parsley or chopped chives can be used as an extra garnish.

divadon'ts

Don't top the crostini more than 1 hour in advance. Don't leave the assembled crostini in direct sunlight.

golden shallot pancakes with garlic and green-olive tapenade

● Makes 25 pancakes to serve 10–12   ● Preparation: 30 minutes   ● Cooking: 20 minutes

The sweet, velvety shallots provide a great base for the sharp, gutsy tapenade.

shallot pancakes

1 tablespoon (½ oz) butter

6 shallots, thinly sliced

1 medium egg

⅓ cup plus 1 tablespoon
(3 fl oz) milk

¾ cup (3 oz) sifted self-rising flour

1 oz freshly grated
Parmesan cheese

salt and pepper

pinch of freshly grated nutmeg

tapenade

1 tablespoon olive oil

3 garlic cloves, crushed or chopped

circa 1 cup (7 oz) pitted green olives

2 teaspoons grated lemon zest

2 tablespoons balsamic vinegar

2 tablespoons chopped flat-leaf
(Italian) parsley

garnish

1 tub of bocconcini
(mini-mozzarella), sliced

salt and pepper

1 small handful of fresh basil leaves,
cut into julienne strips

1 teaspoon olive oil

1 To make the pancakes, melt the butter in a non-stick frying pan. Add the shallots and cook until golden. Whisk the egg and milk together, then add the shallots, flour, Parmesan cheese, salt, pepper, and nutmeg, and mix.

2 Drop 4 separate teaspoons of the mixture into the butter in the frying pan. Cook for several minutes until golden brown on both sides and firm to the touch. Repeat until the batter is used up. Set aside until needed.

3 For the tapenade, preheat the olive oil in a frying pan and sauté the garlic until golden brown. Allow to cool, then place with all the remaining ingredients in a food processor or blender. Pulse until chunky.

4 Marinate the sliced bocconcini cheese with salt and pepper, the basil leaves, and olive oil.

5 To assemble, arrange the shallot pancakes on a serving plate and place ½ teaspoon of the tapenade on top. Garnish with a slice of marinated bocconcini.

diva**dos**

Red onions can be used instead of shallots, but shallots are far sweeter. If bocconcini is not available, use chopped mozzarella. Rinse the olives in hot water before use to remove brine, then drain.

The pancakes can be made a day ahead and reheated. The tapenade can be made several days ahead, covered, and kept in a cool place.

Use a good-quality non-stick frying pan. Be sure to brown the pancakes properly on both sides to cook out the floury flavor.

The pancakes can be served cold and topped 1 hour before serving. If serving warm, heat in the oven at 300°F for 15 minutes.

diva**don'ts**

Don't use white onions – they're too watery.

sun-blush tomato pesto with pita breadsticks

- Makes 24 canapés to serve 10   • Preparation: 20 minutes   • Cooking: 15 minutes

Long pita breadsticks are dipped in a piquant dip of sun-blush tomatoes, hot chili paste, and Parmesan cheese. Perfect as a sophisticated canapé or a casual dip.

pesto

1¼ cups (9 oz) sun-blush tomatoes, drained of oil (sun-dried tomatoes in oil can be substituted)

6 oz freshly grated Parmesan cheese

⅔ cup (4½ oz) pine nuts, toasted

1 garlic clove, peeled

2 tablespoons harissa or other chili paste

1 teaspoon each salt and pepper

½ cup (4 fl oz) extra-virgin olive oil

pita breadsticks

2 garlic cloves, crushed

4 tablespoons olive oil

6 large white pita breads

2 tablespoons thyme leaves

1½ teaspoons salt

1 teaspoon pepper

1 Combine all the pesto ingredients, except for the oil, in a food processor. Once finely chopped, slowly add the oil until it is combined. Adjust seasoning to taste.

2 To make the pita breadsticks, preheat the oven to 350°F. Stir the garlic into the oil. Slice the pita breads lengthwise into long, thin strips. Snip the end of each strip to separate. Place the pita strips in a large baking or roasting pan, drizzle with the garlic oil, and toss to coat evenly. Sprinkle with thyme, salt, and pepper. Bake until crisp and golden brown, about 15 minutes, shaking the pan occasionally. Cool on a rack.

3 To serve, place the pesto in a bowl, and serve with baskets of the crispy pita sticks.

diva**dos**

Make the pita breadsticks up to 2 days ahead, but store them in an airtight container. Make the pesto up to 2 days ahead, and keep in the refrigerator.

Make as a dip for more casual parties. Place breadsticks standing up in a large glass, with the pesto in a shallow bowl. Serve the dip with the homemade Diva Breadsticks (with garlic and rosemary confit or red onion and prosciutto) on page 158.

spiced chicken empanaditas with green chili sauce

● Makes 20 canapés to serve 10   ● Preparation: 1 hour   ● Cooking: 25 minutes

Attractive and highly addictive, empanaditas really get a party going! Serve as an hors d'oeuvre, finger food, or as an appetizer.

green chili sauce

1 ripe avocado, peeled, pitted and chopped

2 green chilies, deseeded

1 small handful of cilantro

2 green onions, chopped

1 tablespoon olive oil

grated zest and juice of 1 lime

salt and pepper

1 garlic clove

pastry

1¼ cups (6 oz) all-purpose flour

2 tablespoons (1 oz) butter

a pinch of salt

sunflower oil for deep-frying

filling

1 tablespoon sunflower oil

½ medium onion, finely chopped

3 garlic gloves, finely chopped

6 oz chicken breast meat (approx. 1 breast), finely chopped

½ teaspoon crushed red chilies

½ teaspoon ground cumin

¼ teaspoon ground cinnamon

a pinch of ground cloves

½ cup (4 fl oz) tomato juice

1 teaspoon tomato paste

10 pitted green olives, finely chopped

2 tablespoons raisins

salt and pepper

1 For the green chili sauce, place all the ingredients in a food processor and purée, then adjust seasoning to taste. If your limes are dry, you may need to add more lime juice.

2 To make the pastry, place the flour, butter, and salt in a food processor and pulse until the mixture resembles fine breadcrumbs. Add enough warm water (about ⅓ cup) to make a soft dough. Roll out on a lightly floured surface using a floured rolling pin. Using a 3-inch cookie cutter, stamp out 20 rounds. Chill.

3 For the filling, heat the oil in a large frying pan and sauté the onion and garlic until softened. Add the chicken and stir to break up the lumps while the meat is browning. Add the chili and spices, and stir until the chicken is cooked. Add the tomato juice, tomato paste, olives, and

raisins, and season with salt and pepper. Adjust seasoning to taste. Allow to cool before using.

4 To fill the empanaditas, place a teaspoon of the cold chicken mixture into the center of each pastry round. Using a little water on your fingertips, fold the pastry over the filling to make a half-moon shape, and seal by pinching the edges together. Place the empanaditas in a single layer on a plate or baking sheet, and keep chilled until ready to deep-fry.

5 Heat the oil in a large pan to 375°F, or preheat a deep-fat fryer. Fry 4 empanaditas at a time for 5 minutes. Drain well on paper towels and keep warm in a low oven.

6 To serve, arrange on a serving plate, with the green chili sauce in a dipping bowl.

diva**dos**

Chop the raw chicken by dicing and placing in the food processor to purée. Pork, white fish, or shrimp can be used instead of chicken.

The pastry and filling can be made a day ahead, the sauce 6 hours ahead, and the empanaditas filled and refrigerated 6 hours ahead.

diva**don'ts**

Don't fill the empanaditas while the filling is still warm. Don't fry too many at once – the oil temperature will drop and the pastry will become soggy.

Don't pile the uncooked empanaditas on top of each other, as they will stick.

warm roquefort wontons

● Makes 20 canapés to serve 10   ● Preparation: 45 minutes   ● Cooking: 10 minutes

Everyone loves crunchy wontons with tasty fillings. This one will take your guests by surprise, since we've combined the crispy wrapper with a delicious, creamy, cheese-and-herb filling.

filling

4 oz ricotta cheese

3 oz Roquefort cheese

grated zest of ½ lemon

1 large handful of basil leaves, chopped

3 green onions, finely chopped

salt and pepper

a pinch of freshly grated nutmeg

wontons

40 wonton wrappers

sunflower oil for deep-frying

1 Mash the wonton filling ingredients together with a large fork. Place in a bowl, cover and chill for at least 30 minutes.

2 Take 1 wonton wrapper, brush with a little water and place another wrapper on top. Spoon a small teaspoon of the mixture in the center, then dampen the edges with a little water. Bring the edges up into the shape of an old-fashioned purse or a traditional pasta tortellini. Repeat with the remaining wrappers and the mixture.

3 Heat the oil in a large pan to 375°F, or preheat a deep-fat fryer, and fry the wontons in batches of about 5 until golden. Keep warm in a medium hot oven until ready to serve.

diva**dos**

 Use fresh thyme instead of basil in the filling, if desired.

 The wontons can be filled 1 hour beforehand, then chilled in a single layer. The filling could be made the day ahead, covered and chilled.

You could serve the wontons with a spicy, roasted-tomato dip. Arrange them on a large, brightly painted plate with wedges of lemon.

The wontons can be fried and kept warm for an hour before serving.

diva**don'ts**

Don't allow the filled wontons to become too warm before frying, or the cheese mixture will leak out. Don't use too much water when wrapping the wontons or they will get too soggy.

mini caesar salads en croûte

● Makes 20 canapés to serve 10   ● Preparation: 20 minutes   ● Cooking: 10 minutes

Everyone loves Caesar salad. But what transforms this version from
the classic-yet-common to the downright-diva-delectable is its stunning
miniature presentation.

Caesar dressing

2 egg yolks

1 teaspoon Dijon mustard

1 garlic clove, peeled

2 anchovy fillets (fresh, canned in olive
oil or salted) optional

1 tablespoon white wine vinegar

1 teaspoon sugar

salt and pepper

½ cup plus 2 tablespoons (5 fl oz)
sunflower oil

½ oz freshly grated
Parmesan cheese

croûtes and salad

7 pieces of thinly sliced white bread

3 tablespoons olive oil

10 anchovies (as above)

a little milk

1 heart of a romaine lettuce

20 Parmesan cheese shavings

a handful of chives, chopped

1 For the dressing, place the
egg yolks, mustard, garlic, anchovies,
vinegar, sugar, salt, and pepper
in a food processor. Slowly drizzle
in the oil while blending to form a
thick, creamy dressing. Stir in the
grated Parmesan cheese.

2 To make the croûtes, preheat the
oven to 400°F. Place the bread slices
on a flat surface and remove the
crusts. Flatten by rolling a heavy
rolling pin over the bread several
times. Using a square or round 2-inch
cookie cutter, cut out 3 croûtes per
slice of bread, ending up with
approximately 20. Push each croûte
into a mini-muffin pan. Brush the

inside of each with olive oil and bake
in the preheated oven for 8 minutes,
or until golden brown (they might need
another 2 minutes – depending on
the oven).

3 To assemble the salad, slice
each anchovy in half lengthwise and
soak in a little milk. Drain and pat
dry with paper towels. Slice the
lettuce thinly and gently toss with
the Caesar dressing. Place a
teaspoon of salad into each croûte.

4 Garnish each with a shaving
of Parmesan cheese, some chives,
and a slice of anchovy.

diva**dos**

Make the croûtes well ahead of
time; store in an airtight container.

Soaking the anchovies in milk for up
to 10 minutes removes the strong
fishy flavor so many people dislike.

Go for all-out sophistication and
garnish each croûte with a soft-
boiled quail's egg.

diva**don'ts**

Don't dress the salad more than
an hour before serving. There is
nothing more unpalatable than
a soggy Caesar!

spiced corn cakes with avocado-lime salsa

● Makes 20 canapés to serve 10   ● Preparation: 35 minutes   ● Cooking: 10 minutes

These slightly spicy, colorful little corn cakes and fresh avocado salsa make a delectable combination.

corn cakes

3 tablespoons yellow cornmeal

½ cup (2 oz) all-purpose flour

sea salt

¼ teaspoon baking powder

1 egg, beaten

add more liquid

½ c. ~~3 tablespoons~~ milk

1 tablespoon butter, melted

½ teaspoon dried chili flakes

2 green onions, finely chopped

½ cup (4 oz) corn kernels, fresh or canned

cayenne pepper

3 tablespoons sunflower oil

avocado-lime salsa

1 avocado, peeled, pitted, and finely diced

½ medium red onion, finely chopped

juice of 1 lime

1 tablespoon olive oil

salt and pepper

a dash of Tabasco sauce

to serve

cilantro

1 To prepare the corn cakes, mix all the ingredients, except the oil, in a large bowl. Heat 1 tablespoon of oil in a non-stick frying pan. Drop the mixture by teaspoons into the frying pan (it should hold about 5 at a time). After about a minute, flip them over; cook until browned on both sides. Repeat with the remaining mixture, using more oil as required. Cool.

2 To make the salsa, simply mix the salsa ingredients together, and adjust seasoning to taste.

3 To assemble, top each corn cake with a teaspoon of avocado-lime salsa and a cilantro leaf.

diva**dos**

Use fresh corn kernels when in season.

Make the corn cakes a day ahead, but keep chilled in an airtight container. Bring back to room temperature to serve, or reheat them for 5 minutes in a hot oven.

Use a large, ridged griddle pan to cook the cakes. Use a spatula along with a teaspoon to gently turn the cakes over.

Serve on a bamboo mat or plate lined with a banana leaf.

diva**don'ts**

Don't make the salsa too far in advance. Prepare a couple of hours before serving and cover tightly with plastic wrap.

Don't undercook the cakes; otherwise they will fall apart when picked up.

smoked salmon on toasted bread with parsley-caper salsa

● Makes 20 canapés to serve 10   ● Preparation: 20 minutes

This sensational combination of ingredients is easy to prepare – and pure elegance to eat.

5 slices of rye bread, toasted

2 oz cream cheese

smoked salmon (about 3½ oz) cut into strips

pepper

parsley-caper salsa

1 tablespoon baby capers

1 small handful of fresh flat-leaf (Italian) parsley, finely chopped

2 green onions, finely chopped

1 tablespoon olive oil

grated zest of ½ lemon

½ teaspoon Dijon mustard

1 To make the salsa: drain, rinse, and dry the capers, then mix them with the chopped parsley, chopped green onion, olive oil, lemon zest, and mustard. Taste and adjust the seasoning accordingly.

2 Spread the cream cheese evenly over the toasted rye bread and cut

each piece of toast into 4 even pieces (use a shaped cookie cutter if preferred).

3 Arrange the smoked salmon in a little mound on each piece of toast and pile a spoonful of the salsa on top. Garnish with freshly ground black pepper.

diva**dos**

Substitute smoked salmon for smoked trout. Try using other breads, such as rye, olive, or caraway. Finely chopped shallots can replace the green onion.

The bread can be toasted up to 4 hours ahead. The salsa can be prepared up to 6 hours ahead and kept covered and chilled.

The salsa makes an excellent topping for crostini. You can also garnish with sprigs of fresh dill.

diva**don'ts**

Don't assemble more than 1 hour in advance. Don't make the salsa too runny – it should be of spooning consistency.

smoked salmon in filo cups with roasted pepper and dill salsa

● Makes 20 canapés to serve 10   ● Preparation: 45 minutes   ● Cooking: 10 minutes

Delicate filo tartlets filled with a silky combination of salmon, roasted peppers, dill, and lime – the perfect complement for other Mediterranean courses.

filo tartlets

12 filo pastry sheets

2 tablespoons (1 oz) butter, melted

salmon and salsa filling

5 oz smoked salmon, cut into slices

1 red pepper and 1 yellow pepper

¼ cup extra-virgin olive oil

1 tablespoon balsamic vinegar

1 garlic clove, finely chopped

6 basil leaves, finely chopped

1 lime, peeled, segmented and halved

2 tablespoons chopped dill

1 teaspoon each of salt and pepper

½ cup (4 fl oz) crème fraîche

1 To make the tartlets, preheat the oven to 350°F, and follow instruction 1 on page 37. Carefully remove the tartlets from the pans and cool on racks.

2 To make the filling, blacken the peppers under the broiler until dark on all sides. Place in a plastic bag and leave for 5 minutes. Remove from the bag, peel away the skin, and discard the seeds and stems. Dice the pepper flesh and place in a small bowl. Add the oil, vinegar, garlic, basil, halved lime segments, dill, salt, and pepper. Leave to marinate for at least an hour.

3 To assemble, place 1 teaspoon crème fraîche into each tartlet, place a swirl of salmon on top, add 1 teaspoon of the pepper salsa, and garnish with extra dill or basil.

divados

Be sure to use a good-quality smoked salmon – or you could substitute smoked trout.

Make the salsa the night before and refrigerate. You can make the filo tartlets at least a week before and keep them in an airtight container.

Try serving the salsa with a smoked-salmon salad as an appetizer, along with rye or walnut bread.

divadon'ts

Don't assemble the tartlets more than half an hour ahead, or the pastry will get soggy.

garnishes

As much attention should be paid to food presentation as to its flavor. Some go so far as to say presentation is the most important aspect of good cooking, but we don't completely agree with that statement. Imagine how disappointing it would be bite into a spectacular-looking dish, only to be greeted by dull and uninteresting flavors!

CHILIES

A vibrant garnish for canapés, salads, barbecued foods, and oriental dishes. Choose long, not tiny or balloon-shaped chilies, as the latter are too hot. Cut in half lengthwise, and run a teaspoon down the inside to remove the seeds. Lay the chili flat on a chopping board and, using a small serrated knife, slice into very thin strips. Arrange 3 to 4 strips into appropriate dishes. Keep, chilled and covered, for one day.

OVEN-DRIED CHERRY TOMATOES

Serve in salads, with hot vegetables, to garnish roasted meats, and to top crostini. Cut in half, lay on a baking sheet, and drizzle with olive oil and balsamic vinegar, sprinkle with salt and pepper, and roast for 30 minutes in an oven preheated to 350°F. Cool and store in one layer in a plastic container.

PICKLED GINGER

Normally served with fresh sushi, this bright-pink garnish can be found in some supermarkets and most oriental food stores. It is an attractive decoration for most oriental foods, providing good flavor and vibrant color. We slice it thinly and stack it on dishes such as canapés, noodle salads, salmon, or Asian marinated fish. Keep pickled ginger in its jar in a cool place.

ROSEMARY SKEWERS

The rosemary flavor spreads through the skewered, usually barbecued, food. Choose long, firm rosemary stems. Pull off all the leaves, leaving half an inch of leaves at the tip of the stalk for garnish. Carve a sharp end to aid skewering the food. Prepare 2 days beforehand.

FRESH HERBS

Herbs provide a light, fresh way to garnish any dish. We recommend basil, flat-leaf (Italian) parsley, dill, cilantro, rosemary, thyme, chives, oregano, chervil, and Thai basil. "Chiffonade" basil leaves by stacking 4 on top of each other; roll up tightly and slice very thinly. Chop chives finely or into long, diagonal pieces. Use whole cilantro or parsley sprigs and leaves. Deep-fry thyme sprigs and sage leaves to garnish warm winter salads, pastas, and roasts. To keep fresh, store in a cool, moist, airy place.

GREEN ONION JULIENNE

Extra-thin, these are incredibly versatile for oriental and Mediterranean dishes. Trim and slice in half lengthwise. Cut into julienne strips lengthwise or diagonally into thin slices. If you require tiny curled julienne strips, place in ice water. Prepare 1 day ahead.

CITRUS FRUIT

Citrus fruits add flavor as well as color. We use segments, grated zest or julienne rind.

Segmenting citrus fruits: Cut away the rind and pith. Slide a knife down one side of each segment, cutting it away from the skin. Cut down the other side and pull out the segment. Store in a sealed container for up to 2 days. Delicious with smoked fish, salads or desserts.

Cutting julienne strips: With a potato peeler, peel the rind off the fruit, leaving the pith behind, or scrape the pith off the back of the rind with a serrated knife. Stack several strips on top of each other and cut them into very thin julienne strips. They can be served raw or you can blanch them in boiling water for 1 minute to soften. Store in a plastic container. Use on savory or sweet dishes.

CUCUMBER CUPS AND RIBBONS

Cucumber cups: Light, fresh, and elegant, use these for canapés with a variety of fillings (see pages 28–29). Store in one layer, covered and chilled, for up to a day. Fill no more than 1 hour before serving.

Cucumber ribbons: Peel the cucumber with a vegetable peeler, and discard the skin. Run the peeler down the cucumber in order to create long, thin ribbons. Keep in the fridge for up to 4 hours. A good garnish for oriental dishes or to toss with other ingredients for a salad.

TOASTED SESAME SEEDS

We use these to give a light, nutty crunch to many foods, especially canapés, noodle salads, and Middle Eastern desserts. They are quick and easy to use and will not soften like herbs do. You must be careful when toasting, however, as they burn easily. Preheat the oven to 350°F. Scatter the seeds onto a flat baking sheet and toast for 7 minutes until evenly browned. Alternatively, toast them in a frying pan over a medium heat, stirring several times. They keep well in a sealed container.

PARMESAN CHEESE SHAVINGS

Start with a large hunk of Parmesan cheese. Use a potato peeler or a serrated knife and peel away the cheese in long, thin sheets. Carefully place on a plate and store in the fridge for several days. A great garnish for salads, soups, crostini, or bruschetta.

GINGER JULIENNE

A useful garnish for oriental canapés, Asian meat dishes, poultry, soups, and desserts. Choose really fresh ginger with skin that is shiny and moist – not dry and hairy. Peel away the hard skin and slice the flesh into thin, uniform strips. Pile the strips on top of each other and cut in julienne. They can be stored in a covered container, chilled, for several days.

CROSTINI/TOASTED BREADS

Crostini should be made from the thinnest French bread you can find. A day-old stick works best. Slice the bread into half-inch discs, brush with olive oil, sprinkle with sea salt, and place on a baking sheet. Place in an oven preheated to 350°F for 10 minutes until lightly golden and crisp. Make up to 2 weeks in advance and store in an airtight container. Serve plain, topped, or with salads and soups.

JAPANESE SESAME SEEDS

Buy these already mixed in bottles from supermarkets and oriental food stores. "Japanese Seasoning" includes white and black sesame seeds, nori (seaweed), and red *shiso* leaves. This provides a delicious, nutty, slightly salty, and colorful garnish.

sri lankan fish cakes with tomato sambal

● Makes 20 canapés to serve 10   ● Preparation: 45 minutes   ● Cooking: 20 minutes

After a wonderful visit to Sri Lanka, we brought many culinary inspirations home. This recipe is adapted from the fish cakes made for us daily by a very gifted cook we were fortunate enough meet during our stay.

2 tablespoons vegetable oil

5½ oz cooked flaked fish (tuna, haddock or cod)

2 shallots, finely chopped

1½ cups (6 oz) mashed potato

1 green chili, chopped (more if you prefer spicy food)

4 curry leaves, chopped

salt and pepper

a good pinch of cayenne pepper

grated zest and juice of 1 lime

2 eggs, beaten

1 cup fine fresh breadcrumbs

sunflower oil for deep-frying

tomato sambal

6 ripe tomatoes

1 red onion, finely diced

1 green chili, finely chopped

juice of 1 lemon

1 tablespoon olive oil

salt and pepper

1 To start the sambal, cut an X at the bottom of each tomato and dip into a pan of boiling water until the skin starts to peel back. Immediately place the tomatoes in a bowl of cold water and slip off the loose skin. Cut the tomatoes in half and scoop out the seeds. Chop the tomato flesh finely and add the red onion, green chili, lemon juice, olive oil, and some salt and pepper. Set aside.

2 To make the fish cakes, heat the oil in a large saucepan and add all the fish-cake ingredients, except for the lime zest and juice, eggs, breadcrumbs, and sunflower oil. Cook over a medium heat for a

few minutes. Mash the ingredients together with a large wooden spoon. Add the lime zest and juice, and season to taste. Form little balls and roll in egg and then breadcrumbs. Chill.

3 To cook, Heat the oil in a large pan to 375°F, or preheat a deep-fat fryer, and fry 5 cakes at a time until golden. Drain well on paper towels, and keep warm in a medium oven. Serve warm with the tomato sambal.

divados

Add cilantro to the fish cakes for variety.

The fish cakes can be made the day before, as can the tomato sambal. Chill and cover.

Serve sprinkled with sea salt and large wedges of fresh lime.

divadon'ts

Don't add the seasoning and lemon juice to the sambal until 1 hour before serving.

Don't deseed the chili, since this is the true Sri Lankan flavor.

asian salmon on star toast with chili crème fraîche

- Makes 25 canapés to serve 10–12 • Preparation: 3 days' marinating and 30 minutes

Making your own gravlax couldn't be easier and more elegant. Once the fish has marinated, you simply slice and serve.

salmon

2 tablespoons sugar

2 tablespoons salt

1 lb 2 oz salmon fillet, with skin (1 center-cut piece)

1-inch piece of fresh root ginger, peeled and grated

1 lemongrass stalk, lower parts only, hard layers removed, finely chopped

grated rind of 1 lime

½ teaspoon coriander seeds, toasted and ground

1 teaspoon black pepper

1 red chili, deseeded, finely chopped

3 tablespoons finely chopped cilantro

1 tablespoon finely chopped mint

chili crème fraîche

1 cup (approx. 7 fl oz) crème fraîche

1 tablespoon finely chopped mint

2 small red chilies, deseeded and finely diced

juice of 1 lime

2 tablespoons chopped cilantro

salt and pepper

to serve

12–14 pieces white bread

1 small cucumber, deseeded and finely diced

cilantro leaves

julienne strips of deseeded red chili

1 To prepare the salmon, combine the sugar and salt and rub into both sides of the salmon. Mix the remaining salmon ingredients together and paste all over the fish. Wrap tightly in plastic wrap. Place on a small cutting board and top with another board. Weight down with heavy cans or weights, and leave in the refrigerator for 3 days, turning the fish over twice.

2 When the salmon has cured, remove the wrapping and wipe off any excess marinade. Place on a wooden board and use a sharp, long, narrow knife to slice. Hold the knife almost parallel to the fish and slice ⅛-inch thick.

3 For the chili crème fraîche, mix all the ingredients together, seasoning to taste, and refrigerate.

4 For the toasts, preheat the oven to 400°F. Using a star-shaped cookie cutter, cut out 2 stars from each slice. Place on a baking sheet and bake for 8 minutes, turning the toasts over once.

5 To assemble, top each toast with 1 teaspoon chili crème fraîche, and curl a slice of salmon around on the top. Garnish with cucumber, a cilantro leaf, and julienne chili.

divados

Check the salmon for any remaining bones, and remove with tweezers. Substitute the fresh tuna for salmon, if desired.

Make the chili crème fraîche and star toasts the day before, but keep the toasts in an airtight container.

Serve on its own as an appetizer or impressive brunch dish.

divadon'ts

Don't slice the salmon until the day of the party, and remember to sharpen your knife beforehand.

shrimp, mint, and ginger spring rolls

● Makes 25 canapés to serve 10 –12   ● Preparation: 1 hour

Unlike their deep-fried cousins from China, Thai spring rolls are made from a rice-paper wrapper that's soaked in water before rolling. The result is a fresh, healthy snack that is full of Southeast Asian flavors. Serve with peanut sauce as a dip.

½ pound medium shrimp, cooked and peeled

2 medium red onions, thinly sliced

2 large carrots, cut into julienne strips

1 x 4-inch piece of daikon (white radish), cut into julienne strips (optional)

1 x 3-inch piece fresh root ginger, cut into julienne strips

12 cilantro sprigs, about 3-inches long

24 Thai basil leaves (or ordinary basil)

24 mint leaves

12 circular rice-paper wrappers (6 inches in diameter)

peanut sauce

1 teaspoon vegetable oil

1½ teaspoons chopped garlic

1 teaspoon crushed red chili or chili bean paste

¼ cup (2 fl oz) hoisin sauce

2 tablespoons smooth peanut butter

1 teaspoon tomato paste

1 teaspoon sugar

¼ cup (2 fl oz) water

1 Place the shrimp, onion, carrots, daikon (white radish), and ginger in separate piles on a plate. Set out the fresh herbs in small stacks.

2 Place a large, clean dish towel on your work surface. Pour hot water into a bowl. Drop one rice-paper wrapper at a time into the water for about 30 seconds. When soft and pliable, place the wrapper on the dish towel and wipe off excess water with another towel.

3 Place 2 mint leaves on the top part of the wrapper. Place 4 shrimp across the wrapper's diameter (make sure they are on the lower part of the wrapper). Place a small amount of the onion, carrot, white radish, and ginger, a cilantro sprig, and 2 basil leaves over the shrimp. Bring up the lower front of the rice paper over the vegetables and then fold the sides in. Roll up the front side until it's a tight spring roll. Place seam-side down on a dish towel. Try to roll it as tight as possible without ripping the wrapper.

Throw away any wrapper that rips and start again with a fresh one. It may take a few to get the knack, so don't be discouraged. If the wrapper is too soft, it will fall apart, and if it's too hard, it will not stick together. Practice a few to get a feel for the right consistency.

4 When ready to serve, cut each spring roll in half diagonally with a very sharp knife. Place on a plate with a sushi mat, which makes an attractive presentation, or on a platter scattered with extra cilantro and mint leaves. Pour the peanut sauce into a small bowl and serve on the side.

peanut sauce

1 Heat the oil in a small saucepan. Add the garlic and crushed chili or bean paste and stir for 5 seconds.

2 Pour the mixture into a small bowl with the rest of the ingredients, and stir until smooth.

diva**dos**
Try Thai food stores, if possible, for rice-paper wrappers and Thai basil, or look carefully in your local supermarket.

diva**don'ts**
Don't make the spring rolls more than 6 hours in advance.

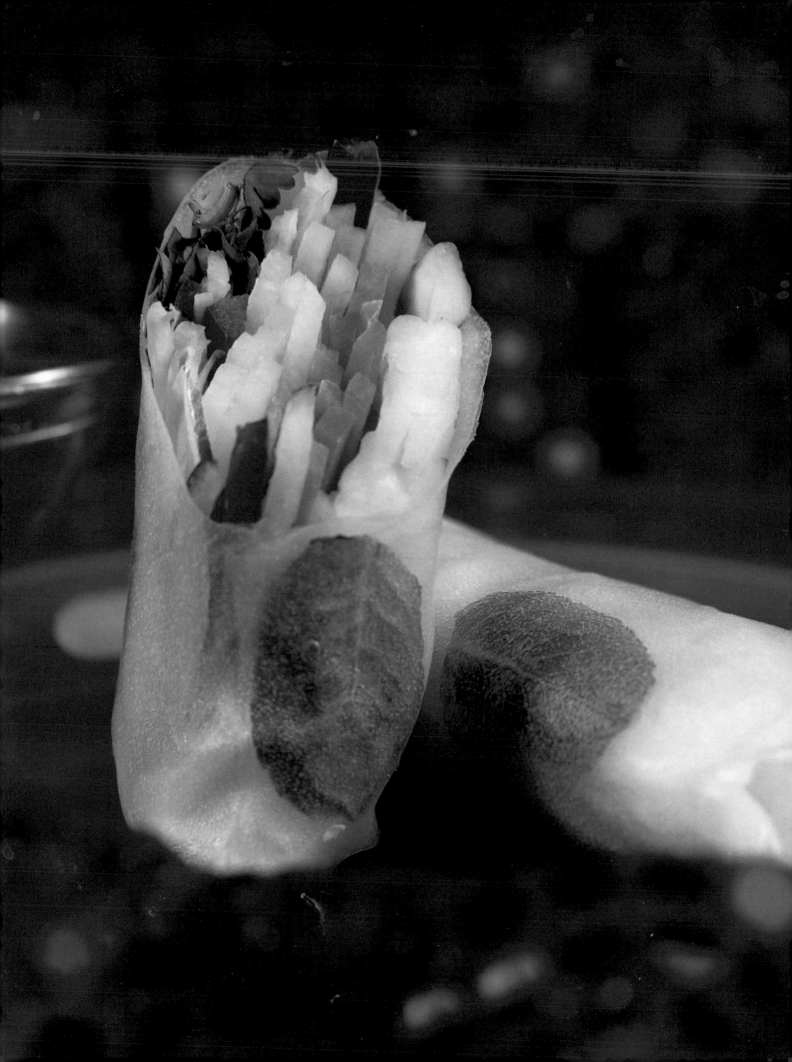

crispy crab and cream cheese wontons

- Makes 20 canapés to serve 10   • Preparation: 25 minutes   • Cooking: 10 minutes

Crispy wontons with creamy hot cheese and crab are dipped into a sweet chili sauce – it's pure decadence!

6 oz fresh or canned crab meat – white meat only!

8 oz cream cheese

2 green onions, thinly sliced

1 small red chili, deseeded and diced

salt and pepper

40 wonton wrappers

1 egg white

vegetable oil for deep-frying

Thai sweet chili sauce

1 Mix the crab, cream cheese, green onions, chili, salt, and pepper in a small mixing bowl.

2 Place half the wonton wrappers on a clean dish towel with the corners facing towards you. Brush each wonton with egg white. Place a second wonton on top of the brushed wonton, creating a double thickness. Place a teaspoon of the crab filling in the lowest corner of the wonton; brush egg white around all sides. Fold the wrapper over the filling (it should look like a triangle at this point). Take the top 2 corners of the wrapper and pinch together into a tortellini shape. Brush with more egg white to seal, if needed. Repeat with the remaining wontons.

3 Heat the oil in a large heavy saucepan to 375°F, or until a small piece of bread sizzles instantly. Fry 5 wontons at a time until crisp, then drain well on paper towels.

4 Serve immediately with the Thai sweet chili sauce.

divados

If you can find it, buy a large bottle of Thai sweet chili sauce from an Asian supermarket. It keeps well, and is delicious on anything fried. You can replace the crab meat with chopped cooked shrimp.

The wontons can be deep-fried ahead of time and reheated in the oven at 400°F for 5 minutes.

divadon'ts

Ensure that the oil is hot enough, otherwise the wontons will be soggy. Use a deep-fat fryer if possible, or a thick-based, heavy saucepan.

spicy shrimp with moroccan tomato jam

- Makes 24 canapés to serve 12   • Preparation: 10 minutes   • Cooking: 1 hour

Large, juicy shrimp grilled with a delicious spicy tomato jam: the perfect food to start an exotic evening. You will need 24 wooden skewers, which you should soak in water for an hour before using.

24 jumbo shrimp,
peeled and deveined

24 x 2-inch pieces of green onion

1 tablespoon clear honey

a small handful of
cilantro, chopped

moroccan tomato jam

2 garlic cloves, finely chopped

2 tablespoons finely chopped
fresh root ginger

2 tablespoons olive oil

½ cup cider vinegar

1 cinnamon stick

1 x 28-oz can peeled plum tomatoes,
chopped or puréed

4 tablespoons soft brown sugar

1 teaspoon ground cumin

½ teaspoon cayenne pepper

⅛ teaspoon ground cloves

salt and pepper

1 Sauté the garlic and ginger in the olive oil for 2 minutes. Add the vinegar and cinnamon stick, and cook for 1 minute. Stir in the remaining ingredients. Reduce the heat and cook gently until all the liquid has evaporated, about 1 hour. Keep an eye on it to prevent burning. Remove the cinnamon. Allow to cool to room temperature.

2 Preheat a broiler or barbecue. Coat the shrimp with tomato jam and place one on each skewer with a piece of green onion. Drizzle with the honey, and grill for 1 minute each side.

3 Sprinkle with the chopped cilantro and serve with the remaining jam.

diva**dos**

Make the jam up to a week ahead, and refrigerate. Skewer the shrimp in the morning and chill.

Arrange the skewers standing up on the platter, resting on the shrimp. Serve with dishes like Filo Tart with Charmoula Chicken or Couscous with Roasted Sweet Potato (see pages 52 and 105).

diva**don'ts**

Don't forget to soak the skewers – otherwise, they will catch light and you will have a small bonfire under your broiler!

cucumber cups with thai shrimp

● Makes 20 canapés to serve 10   ● Preparation: 30 minutes

This is the fastest canapé you can possibly make. These little cucumber cups can be used with all kinds of delectable fillings, but we think the shrimp with chili sauce is the best.

2 large, long cucumbers

4½ oz medium shrimp, cooked and shelled

1 small handful of cilantro, chopped

6 tablespoons Thai sweet chili sauce

toasted sesame seeds to garnish (optional)

1 To make the cucumber cups, cut the cucumbers into 20 x 2-inch thick slices. Stamp each slice with a suitably sized crinkled pastry cutter, removing the cucumber skin. Using a melon baller or teaspoon, make a hollow in the center of the cucumber cups to nestle your filling in.

2 Drain the shrimp and pat dry. Place in a bowl with the chopped cilantro and chili sauce, and mix well.

3 Fill each cucumber cup with chili shrimp, and sprinkle toasted sesame seeds (if using) on top.

divados

A mousse made from blue cheese mixed well with cream cheese is delicious in these cups, topped with bacon and chives. Or try thin slices of smoked salmon with pickled ginger and wasabi.

The cucumber cups can be made the day before. Chill, covered, on paper towels. The shrimp filling can be mixed together 1 hour before serving.

The cucumber cups are great with any fried foods, as they create such a texture contrast.

divadon'ts

Don't fill the cucumber cups with shrimp more than 30 minutes before serving.

indian pakoras with two dips

● Makes 25 canapés to serve 10-12   ● Preparation: 45 minutes   ● Cooking: 15 minutes

Pakoras are the tempura of India: deep-fried vegetable slices in a spicy batter. They are irresistible with these two dips.

25 slices of any of the following: onion, potato, baby or small eggplant, baby artichokes, green beans or fennel

vegetable oil for deep-frying

batter

2 tablespoons (1 oz) chickpea flour

3 tablespoons (1½ oz) self-rising flour

½ teaspoon garam masala

½ teaspoon ground cumin

½ teaspoon ground turmeric

½ teaspoon chili powder

½ teaspoon salt

cilantro and mint dip

1 cup (8 fl oz) Greek yogurt

1 shallot, finely chopped

1 tablespoon finely grated fresh ginger root

2 small, mild green chilies, deseeded and chopped

1 tablespoon fine-grained sugar

20 mint leaves

1 large handful cilantro

salt and pepper

tamarind dipping sauce

2 tablespoons dried tamarind pulp (in a sticky block), or ½ cup (4 fl oz) bottled tamarind purée

2 tablespoons soft brown sugar

½ teaspoon each of ground cumin, ground fennel seeds, finely grated fresh root ginger, and salt

1 teaspoon lemon juice

1 For the batter, combine the flours, spices, and salt with ½ cup of water and beat until smooth. The batter should be thick, so add additional flour if necessary.

2 Heat the oil to 375°F, or until a piece of bread sizzles instantly.

3 Peel the onion, keeping the root end on. Cut in thin slices lengthwise so there is a bit of root left to hold the layers together. The eggplant should be left unpeeled and sliced thinly. Artichokes should have hard leaves and stems removed and then be sliced thinly. Remove outer leaves from the fennel and slice out the core; slice thinly. Green beans should be topped and tailed and left whole.

4 Dip the pieces of vegetable one at a time into the batter, then drop into the hot oil. Fry up to 6 pieces at a time. Drain on paper towels.

5 Serve immediately with dips in bowls on the side.

cilantro and mint dip

Place all the ingredients in a food processor and process until smooth. Season to taste.

tamarind dip

1 Place the tamarind pulp in a bowl and cover with ½ cup of hot water. Leave to soak until the water cools. Squeeze the pulp until thoroughly dissolved in the water. Strain through a mesh sieve, pushing all the pulp through, and adding a little more water if necessary. Discard the fibers and seeds. If using bottled tamarind purée, then mix with 3 tablespoons of water.

2 Add the remaining ingredients to the tamarind, and stir well.

diva**dos**

If you're lucky enough to have an Indian food store nearby, it will be an treasure-trove of spices and other interesting ingredients. Use baby vegetables when you can find them: they look very glamorous.

Make the pakoras 3 hours ahead and then reheat in the oven at 400°F for 5 minutes. (This also allows time to remove the frying odor from your kitchen.) The tamarind dip can be made a week before, and kept cool. Make the other sauce just before serving.

diva**don'ts**

Don't slice the vegetables too thickly as they won't fry properly.

wonton cups with chinese chicken salad

● Makes 20 canapés to serve 10   ● Preparation: 45 minutes   ● Cooking: 20 minutes

Light, refreshing, and tasty, these wonton cups make an impressive canapé for any occasion.

40 wonton wrappers

peanut oil

Chinese chicken salad

1 boneless, skinless chicken breast

2 tablespoons light soy sauce

1 tablespoon rice vinegar

1 tablespoon sesame oil

1 bunch green onions, finely chopped

1 small handful flat-leaf (Italian) parsley or cilantro, finely chopped

1 To make the wonton cups, preheat the oven to 350°F. Lay the wrappers out and brush very lightly with oil. (An oil spray bottle is better.) Stack 2 wrappers on top of each other at right angles and push into mini-muffin pans. Bake in the preheated oven for 8 minutes, until crisp. Remove from the oven, cool, and store until needed.

2 To make the filling, place the chicken breast in a pan of cold water, cover, bring to a simmer, and cook for 8 minutes. Turn off the heat, and allow the chicken to cool in the liquid.

3 Slice the chicken very thinly and mix with the soy sauce, rice vinegar, sesame oil, green onions, and parsley or cilantro. Taste to check the flavor. Add more soy sauce or vinegar if needed.

4 Fill each crisp wonton cup with the Chinese chicken salad, and serve at room temperature.

diva**dos**

Use good-quality, organic chicken for the salad.

The wonton cups can be made 2 days beforehand and stored in an airtight container. The chicken salad can be cooked the day before, covered and chilled, but don't add the liquid ingredients until 1 hour before serving.

If cooking a larger number of chicken breasts, place in a water-filled roasting pan, cover with foil and cook at 350°F for 20 minutes. Poaching the chicken keeps it moist, which is the best method for this recipe.

Garnish with toasted sesame seeds or red chili, deseeded and cut into julienne strips.

diva**don'ts**

Don't fill the wonton cups with chicken salad until half an hour before serving.

tuna ceviche on corn tortillas with mango salsa

● Makes 24 canapés to serve 12   ● Preparation: 30–60 minutes   ● Cooking: 10 minutes

A perfect and elegant bite for a Latin evening. Lime-marinated tuna mixed with mango salsa is divine when paired with a warm, crunchy tortilla. Don't forget the margaritas!

½ lb fresh
tuna, finely diced

½ cup (4 fl oz) fresh lime juice

vegetable oil for deep-frying

1 packet of 8 corn tortillas, each cut into 3 large wedge shapes

cilantro leaves

mango salsa

1 small fresh red chili, deseeded and chopped, or 1 chipotle pepper in adobo sauce, finely chopped

1 small red onion, finely chopped

1 teaspoon freshly cracked black pepper

1 teaspoon Tequila

1 teaspoon salt

1 handful of cilantro, chopped

1 large ripe mango, peeled, pitted, and finely diced

juice of 2 limes

1 Place the tuna in the lime juice and marinate for 30 to 60 minutes. Drain and mix thoroughly with all the salsa ingredients.

2 Heat the vegetable oil in a large frying pan. Prepare a bowl lined with paper towels. Test the oil: if hot enough, a small piece of tortilla will crisp and bubble very quickly. This is important; otherwise the tortillas will turn greasy when cooked. The chips will cook quickly, so be remove after 30 seconds with a mesh spoon. Drain well on the paper towels. Alternatively, spray the corn tortillas with oil and bake in the oven at 400°F for 8 minutes.

3 To serve, spoon 1 tablespoon of tuna ceviche onto an individual tortilla chip, and place on a plate garnished with cilantro.

diva**dos**

Use extremely good-quality tuna that is ruby red with very little fat marbling. Or try sea bass as an alternative. Select a large mango that is ripe but not mushy. If corn tortillas are not available, you can buy packaged corn tortilla chips.

The mango salsa can be prepared 2 hours before serving, but don't add the lime juice until just before you are ready to serve.

Serve the tuna ceviche in a bowl with a basket of tortilla chips for a more casual setting.

diva**don'ts**

Don't marinate the tuna for over an hour or the fish will become rubbery. Don't mix the tuna with the salsa until an hour before serving, as mango becomes slimy when left too long with lime juice.

gingered chicken cakes with cilantro sauce

● Makes 20 canapés to serve 10   ● Preparation: 25 minutes   ● Cooking: 20 minutes

We stumbled upon this recipe when Thai fish cakes had had their day in every menu and cookbook. This simple recipe is packed full of oriental flavors, and works well as a canapé or, made larger, as an appetizer or main course.

gingered chicken cakes

2 boneless, skinless chicken breasts, chopped

3 tablespoons Thai fish sauce (nam pla)

1 inch fresh root ginger, peeled

3 green onions, chopped

1 garlic clove, chopped

½ teaspoon sea salt

½ teaspoon dried chili flakes

sunflower oil for shallow-frying

cilantro sauce

2 tablespoons classic mayonnaise (see page 118)

1 small handful of cilantro, finely chopped

juice and finely grated zest of 1 lime

1 To make the cilantro sauce, mix the mayonnaise with the cilantro, lime juice, and zest. Cover and chill.

2 For the gingered chicken cakes, place all the chicken cake ingredients, except the oil, in a food processor, and purée until well-combined. Scoop the mixture out into a bowl and shape into 20 small, round cakes.

3 Heat 1 inch of sunflower oil in a large frying pan and brown the cakes for 3 minutes on both sides. Drain on paper towels.

4 Keep warm in a medium oven until ready to eat. Serve with a bowl of the cilantro sauce.

diva**dos**

Use really fresh ginger, otherwise it will become stringy in the food processor (and be unpleasant to eat). Make sure it is well-chopped before combining with the chicken.

The cakes can be made the day before and stored raw, covered, in the fridge. The sauce can keep, covered, for 1 week in the fridge. When shaping the cakes, it helps to have a small bowl of warm water available to dip your fingers in, since this is quite a sticky job!

When making the cakes in large numbers, brown them in a pan and cook through in a hotter oven to save time.

 Thai sweet chili sauce also makes an excellent dip for these little cakes. Serve the cakes on a bamboo mat placed on a white plate. Add a small dipping bowl for the sauce, and garnish with wedges of lime.

diva**don'ts**

Don't overcook the chicken cakes or they will be tough.

vietnamese grilled pork in lettuce parcels

● Makes 24 canapés to serve 12   ● Preparation: 45 minutes   ● Cooking: 15 minutes

These grilled, caramelized balls of ground pork contain all the great Vietnamese flavors. They're delicious served in crunchy lettuce parcels with a chili sauce.

1 lb 2 oz lean ground pork

4 shallots, finely chopped

3 garlic cloves, crushed

2 tablespoons trimmed and finely chopped fresh lemongrass

1½ teaspoons cornstarch

1 tablespoon finely chopped mint

3 tablespoons finely chopped cilantro

4 tablespoons Thai fish sauce (nam pla)

½ teaspoon each of salt and pepper

½ cup (2 oz) sugar

to serve

24 romaine lettuce heart leaves, washed and dried

1 medium cucumber, peeled, deseeded and diced

1 red onion, finely diced

mint and cilantro sprigs

Thai sweet chili sauce

1 In a large bowl, mix together the pork, shallots, garlic, lemongrass, cornstarch, mint, cilantro, fish sauce, salt, and pepper.

2 Preheat the oven to 200°C.

3 With lightly oiled hands, shape the pork mixture into 24 x 1½- to 2-inch balls. (They will shrink while cooking.) Roll each meatball in the sugar, and place on a baking sheet lined with a sheet of waxed paper.

4 Bake in the preheated oven for 15 minutes. Shake the sheet a couple of times while they cook, so that they don't burn on one side.

5 To serve, place a meatball on a lettuce leaf. Add some diced cucumber, onion, and a sprig of mint and cilantro. Drizzle 1 teaspoon of sweet chili sauce over each.

diva**dos**

Make sure the pork is of good quality and lean.

You can prepare the pork balls 3–4 hours in advance. Before serving, reheat in the oven at 400°F for 5 minutes until hot.

Remember when using lemongrass to use the bottom third of the stalk. Smash with the flat side of a knife, and peel off the hard layers. Finely chop the remaining soft piece.

filo tartlets with seared duck and tomato-sesame chutney

- Makes 20 canapés to serve 10 ● Preparation: 1 hour ● Cooking: 1 hour

A sumptuous meal made miniature. Tender pieces of duck are set against a sweet-and-sour chutney – pure heaven!

filo tartlets

12 filo pastry sheets

2 tablespoons (1 oz) butter, melted

duck filling

2 duck breasts

1 tablespoon light soy sauce

1 teaspoon honey

tomato-sesame chutney

½ lb (8 oz) ripe tomatoes

¹¹⁄₃ cup plus 1 tablespoon (3 fl oz) white-wine vinegar

⅓ cup (2–3 oz) sugar

a few fennel seeds

½ teaspoon curry powder

2 cardamom pods, split

a pinch each of cayenne pepper and ground ginger

a small handful of raisins

1 tablespoon sesame seeds, toasted

1 Preheat the oven to 350°F. Brush 1 filo pastry sheet with some of the melted butter. Use a sharp knife to cut the pastry into 2-inch squares. Stack 4 squares at different angles on top of each other, so that the finished stack has a star-like appearance. Push the pastry firmly into a mini-muffin pan to obtain a flat bottom for the tartlets. Repeat this process with the remaining pastry. Bake for 6–8 minutes until golden. Carefully remove from the pans and cool on racks.

2 To start the chutney, skin the tomatoes by cutting an X in the bottom of each. Drop into a pan of boiling water for a minute, then place in a bowl of cold water to refresh for 1 minute before slipping off the skins. Roughly chop the tomatoes.

3 Heat the vinegar and sugar together over a low heat, stirring with a wooden spoon until the sugar

has dissolved. Raise the heat and add all the remaining ingredients except for the sesame seeds. Simmer for approximately 30 minutes until thickened. Cool and remove the cardamom pods. Set aside until needed.

4 Preheat the oven to 400°F. To prepare the duck, remove the skin and fat, if preferred, using a sharp knife to pull it away from the flesh. Brush the duck with the soy sauce and honey. Preheat a frying pan, and sear the duck breast (without any oil) for 2 minutes on each side, then roast for 10 minutes until still pink. Rest and cool.

5 To assemble, slice the duck breasts thinly, and place 2 slices in each tartlet. Top with a teaspoon of chutney, and scatter with toasted sesame seeds.

divados

 Make the tomato-sesame chutney days or weeks in advance. It goes well with many meat and cheese dishes – it's quite valuable for daily diva cooking. The filo tartlets can be made a week ahead and kept in an airtight container. The duck can be cooked the day before.

You can garnish the tartlets with thinly sliced red chili, cilantro leaves or chives.

diva**tarts**

parsley and roasted garlic tart

- Serves: 8   • Preparation: 1 hour   • Cooking: 45 minutes

Any excuse to use roasted garlic will do. By now, you may have guessed that we like it in just about anything!

1 x 8-inch Herb Pastry case,
made with parsley, baked
(see page 48)

olive oil

balsamic vinegar

salt and pepper

filling

3 garlic bulbs

1 cup (8 fl oz) crème fraîche

4 medium eggs

juice and finely grated rind of 1 lemon

¼ – ⅓ cup (½ oz) chives

1 bunch of green onions,
washed and trimmed

2 large handfuls of
flat-leaf (Italian) parsley, chopped

10 cherry plum tomatoes, halved

1 Preheat the oven to 350°F. Place the garlic bulbs on a large piece of foil, drizzle with a little olive oil and tightly seal the foil. Roast for 1 hour. Remove from the oven, open up the foil, and allow to cool. Slice the garlic in half and squeeze out all the roasted pulp. Discard the skins.

2 Place the garlic with all the remaining filling ingredients, except for the tomatoes, in a food processor. Purée. Pour the filling into the tart shell, and arrange the cherry tomato halves on top.

3 Drizzle with olive oil and balsamic vinegar, sprinkle with salt and pepper, and bake in the oven at the same temperature for 45 minutes.

diva**dos**

Basil also works well in this recipe.

The tart can be made a day ahead, and then warmed up to serve.

Purée the filling ingredients well, so that the mixture is bright green.

The recipe can be made into 8 individual tarts. Serve with Tuscan Panzanella Salad or a lovely Baby Green Salad with a tart vinaigrette (see pages 123 and 135).

diva**don'ts**

Don't allow the roasted garlic to get cold; it must be squeezed out while still warm.

caramelized red onion and fennel tarte tatin with olives and thyme

● Serves: 8   ● Preparation: 1 hour   ● Cooking: 40 minutes

Roasted red onion and fennel, perched in flaky puff pastry with a balsamic caramel, is divine for a picnic or a winter dinner.

7–8 oz frozen puff pastry, thawed

filling

6 medium red onions, sliced into thick rings

3 fennel bulbs, each halved, cored and cut into 6 pieces

2 tablespoons olive oil

2 tablespoons balsamic vinegar

2 garlic cloves, finely chopped

salt and pepper

1/4 cup (2 oz) sugar

2 tablespoons water

2 teaspoons chopped thyme

8 olives, pitted and halved

4 oz freshly grated Parmesan cheese

1 Roll out the puff pastry on a floured surface to fit a 9 1/2-inch tart or quiche dish. Place the rolled pastry on a plate and refrigerate for 30 minutes. Line the tart dish with non-stick baking parchment paper. (If using a heavy quiche or tarte tatin pan, you won't need the paper.)

2 Preheat the oven to 350°F. Place the red onions and fennel in a shallow roasting pan. Pour on the olive oil and vinegar, and sprinkle with garlic, salt, and pepper. Try to keep the onion rings intact. Bake for 30 minutes, carefully turning over once during cooking. Set aside to cool.

3 Combine the sugar with the water in a saucepan and stir over a low heat until the sugar dissolves. Bring to a

boil and cook, without stirring, until golden. Pour into the base of the prepared dish.

4 Firmly pack the onion slices, thyme, and olives into the base of the dish. Place the fennel pieces on top and sprinkle with Parmesan cheese. Place the rolled pastry over the filling, and tuck the edges in to fit. Use a fork to prick tiny holes in the pastry to let the steam out.

5 Bake in the oven at the same temperature for 30–40 minutes, until the pastry is puffed and golden. Let the tart cool for 5 minutes before turning out. Run a knife around the edge of the tart, then invert onto a warm plate.

diva**dos**

You could ask your local bakery to sell you some of their puff pastry; this will be a step up from the supermarket variety. Or try making your own.

Prepare the tart the day before, which enhances the flavors and eases turning out.

Indulge in a cast-iron, enamelled tarte tatin pan if your budget is up to it.

diva**don'ts**

Don't stir the caramel while cooking or it will crystallize.

wild mushroom and smoked mozzarella tart

● Serves: 8   ● Preparation: 1 hour   ● Cooking: 45 minutes

Rich, wild mushrooms are set with smoky mozzarella, Parmesan cheese, and a crisp olive crust for the perfect cold-weather tart.

fresh herb and olive pastry

1²/₃ cup (7 oz) all-purpose flour

7 tablespoons (3½ oz) salted butter, chilled and diced

1 small handful flat-leaf (Italian) parsley, basil, oregano or thyme, finely chopped

1 tablespoon black olive paste

1 medium egg

mushroom filling

⅓ cup (1 oz) dried porcini mushrooms

2 tablespoons olive oil

1 large Spanish onion, thinly sliced

2 garlic cloves, chopped

1 lb 2 oz large, dark, wild mushrooms, sliced

4 medium eggs

1¼ cups (10 fl oz) heavy (whipping) cream

1 large handful of flat-leaf (Italian) parsley, chopped

1 large handful of basil, torn (optional)

salt and pepper

freshly grated nutmeg, to taste

4 oz smoked mozzarella, grated or chopped

4 oz freshly grated Parmesan cheese

1 Pulse the flour, butter, and chosen herb in a food processor until the mixture resembles breadcrumbs. Add the black olive paste and egg, and purée until the pastry forms a ball. Place on a floured surface and roll out to line an 8–inch, loose-bottomed pie plate. Chill until required, at least 30 minutes.

2 Preheat the oven to 350°F. Bake the tart shell, following instuctions on page 48 for 10 minutes. Remove the paper and beans and allow to cool for 5 minutes before filling.

3 To make the mushroom filling, soak the dried mushrooms in 1¼ cups boiling water for about 20 minutes. Drain through a piece of cheesecloth to ensure that all dirt and grit is collected, reserving the liquid. Rinse the dried mushrooms and

chop coarsely.

4 Meanwhile, heat the olive oil in a large pan and sauté the onion and garlic until soft. Add the sliced field mushrooms and cook gently for 10 minutes. Add the chopped dried mushrooms with half a cup of the reserved liquid. Remove from heat.

5 Preheat the oven to 375°F.

6 In a large bowl, beat together the eggs, cream, herbs, salt, pepper, and nutmeg. Add the cheeses and mushroom mixture and mix well. Pour into the tart shell and bake in the center of the oven for 45 minutes.

divados

Add other wild mushrooms if you're feeling like a glamorous diva!

Make the pastry shell a day in advance, chill or freeze. Bake at least 6 hours before serving, and reheat to serve.

Serve with Baby Green Salad, Fennel Slaw (see pages 135 and 134), or a warm potato salad with chive and walnut dressing.

divadon'ts

Don't use cultivated white button mushrooms because they simply can't provide the intense flavor a true diva desires!

eggplant, goat cheese, and tomato galette with rocket and basil oil

● Serves: 8   ● Preparation: 45 minutes   ● Cooking: 30 minutes

This tart looks like you've really gone to town, but most of the hard work has been done in advance. It makes a simple and stunning summer starter or light main course.

9 oz frozen puff pastry, thawed

topping

½ cup (4 fl oz) olive oil

1 onion, finely chopped

2 garlic cloves, chopped

1 tablespoon thyme leaves

a good pinch of chopped rosemary leaves

2 medium eggplant, finely diced

¼ lb soft goat cheese

garnishes

1 small handful fresh basil

¼ cup (2 fl oz) olive oil

salt and pepper

6 ripe plum tomatoes

1 teaspoon balsamic vinegar

about 4½ large handfuls (4½ oz) fresh arugula leaves, washed

Parmesan cheese shavings

1 On a lightly floured surface, roll out the pastry to ¼-inch thick. Cut into 8 x 4-inch circles using a cookie cutter. Chill for 30 minutes.

2 Preheat the oven to 400°F.

3 Line a baking sheet with non-stick baking parchment paper and place the pastry circles on top. Prick several times with a fork and bake in for 7 minutes. Turn over, and bake for another 7 minutes until golden and crisp. Leave to cool.

4 For the topping, heat the olive oil in a large pan, add the onion, garlic, thyme, and rosemary, and sauté until soft. Add the eggplant, and cook until everything is softened, about 15 minutes. Check the seasoning and allow to cool slightly before puréeing in a food processor with the goat cheese. Store, covered, in a cool place until needed.

5 To make the basil oil, place the basil, 4 tablespoons of the olive oil, and some salt and pepper into a food processor and blend well. Cover and store until needed.

6 Slice the tomatoes thinly and place in a bowl. Drizzle with the remaining olive oil, the balsamic vinegar, salt, and pepper, and leave to marinate for at least 30 minutes.

7 To assemble the galette, place each pastry circle on a serving plate and spread a spoonful of eggplant mixture on top. Arrange the tomato slices in a neat circle on top and garnish with a few arugula leaves and a large Parmesan cheese shaving. Drizzle the basil oil around the edge of the plate. Serve at room temperature.

diva**dos**

 We use a mild goat cheese, but you could use cream cheese.

The galette can be assembled 1 hour before serving, but add the arugula, Parmesan cheese, and basil oil at the last minute.

 Serve the eggplant purée with our Diva Breadsticks (see page 158).

diva**don'ts**

Don't use large beef tomatoes; they are too watery and less tasty than plum or vine-ripened tomatoes.

winter squash, roasted garlic, and gorgonzola galette

● Serves: 8 ● Preparation: 1 hour ● Cooking: 30 minutes

An excellent vegetarian dish for a cold winter night. Butternut squash gets a touch of glamour from this irresistible combination of roasted garlic, sage, and creamy Gorgonzola cheese!

9 oz puff pastry

1 egg, beaten

filling

2¼ lb butternut squash

olive oil

salt and pepper

1 garlic bulb

1 small onion, finely chopped

10 fresh sage leaves, coarsely chopped

4½ oz Parmesan cheese, freshly grated

3½ oz Gorgonzola cheese, in chunks

1 Preheat the oven to 400°F. Using a large, sharp knife, halve the squash. Scrape out and discard the seeds and fibers using a spoon. Lightly brush each cut side of the squash with olive oil, and season with salt and pepper. Place the squash cut side down on a baking sheet. Tear the garlic bulb apart, but do not peel. Place the cloves under the squash, and drizzle everything with olive oil. Bake for about 1 hour, or until the squash is tender when pierced. Scoop the flesh out into a large bowl. Squeeze the garlic out of its skin and add to the squash.

2 Meanwhile, on a lightly floured surface, roll out the puff pastry into a 13-inch round. Prick the base 6 times with a fork, place the pastry on a flat plate, and chill for 30 minutes.

3 To finish the filling, warm 2 teaspoons of olive oil in a small saucepan over a low heat. Add the onion and sage, and cook until soft. Add to the squash along with the Parmesan cheese. Mash with a wooden spoon or potato masher to combine well. Season with salt and pepper and fold in the Gorgonzola.

4 Preheat the oven to the same temperature. Place a large, flat, slightly oiled baking sheet in to heat. Place the squash filling into the center of the pastry circle, spreading evenly and leaving a 2-inch border. Fold the border over the filling, leaving the center of the filling showing. Brush the overlapping pastry with the beaten egg.

5 To bake the galette, slide it off the plate onto the heated baking sheet. Bake until the crust is nicely browned, about 25 minutes. Serve hot or warm.

diva**dos**

 You could use other blue cheeses, such as Roquefort, for this recipe.

Make the tart filling the day before. Roll out the tart shell the day before. Fill to bake. This galette reheats well.

 Make individual galette tarts for a small gathering – they look very elegant. Serve with a simple green salad topped with a Classic Vinaigrette (see page 118).

smoked fish tart with crème fraîche, lemon, and parmesan

• Serves: 8 • Preparation: 1 hour • Cooking: 25 minutes

We love this creamy, delicate fish tart. Serve warm for lunch with a watercress, chicory, and avocado salad, and a mustard vinaigrette.

lemon and paprika pastry

6 tablespoons (3 oz) butter, chilled and diced

1¼ cups (6 oz) all-purpose flour

grated zest of 1 lemon

a pinch of pepper

½ teaspoon paprika

1 medium egg

filling

1 lb 2 oz undyed smoked haddock, skinned and boned

2 bunches of green onions, trimmed

2 tablespoons (1 oz) butter

2 medium eggs

2 medium egg yolks

1 cup (8 fl oz) crème fraîche

grated zest and juice of 1 lemon

3 oz Parmesan cheese, freshly grated

1 large handful of fresh dill or fennel leaves, chopped

1 To make the pastry, place all the pastry ingredients except the egg in a food processor and blend until the consistency of breadcrumbs. Add the egg and pulse to a dough. If necessary, add a little cold water. Roll out on a lightly floured surface to line a deep, 8- or 9-inch, loose-bottomed tart dish. Chill for 30 minutes.

2 Preheat the oven to 350°F.

3 Bake the pastry case according to instructions on page 48 for 10 minutes. Remove the paper and beans and bake for another 5 minutes to crisp the bottom. Remove from the oven.

4 For the filling, cut the fish and green onions into 1-inch chunks. Melt the butter in a large frying pan, add the onions and sauté until slightly browned. Add the fish and cook for 2 minutes, then spoon this mixture into the tart shell.

5 Whisk together the eggs, egg yolks, crème fraîche, lemon zest and juice, Parmesan cheese, and herbs, and pour over the fish. Bake for 25 minutes, or until just set. Allow to stand for 30 minutes before serving.

divados

Any smoked fish will work well for this recipe. Leeks can be used instead of green onions, but need longer cooking.

The pastry could be made and frozen, uncooked, 1 week before, or refrigerated the day before. The whole tart could be made the day before, then chilled and reheated to serve.

Garnish with chives and wedges of lemon, and serve with a green salad and gutsy dressing (try our Classic Vinaigrette on page 118).

divadon'ts

Don't cook the fish completely in the pan – just brown it, since it will be cooked thoroughly in the oven.

pastry

Making pastry is a lot of fun and with adding extra flavorings, you can vary the classic piecrust and sweet pastry to suit any tart filling. It can be made well ahead and freezes beautifully unbaked. Once the shell is baked, it should be filled and eaten within 24 hours.

CORE INGREDIENTS

Butter: We prefer the flavor of salted butter in sweet and savory pastry. Ensure that the butter is chilled and cut into cubes for making pastry. On warm summer days, it helps to use frozen butter.

Italian 00 Flour: This is the best flour for making pastry because of its fine texture. The Italians use it for making pasta, but not bread, as it is too finely milled. Look for an Italian flour with the "double zero" on the label. It's available now from some supermarkets and speciality shops.

Wholewheat Flour: Wholewheat flour works well mixed with white flour to make a savory, nutty-flavored pastry.

All-purpose flour: If Italian 00 flour is unavailable, use finely milled white flour. Store all flours in their bags on a cool, dry, and airy shelf. They will keep for 6 months.

Sugars: Different sugars can be used for making sweet pastries to vary the flavor and texture. Most often "superfine" sugar, with a finer grain than granulated, is used, but if this isn't available, try whizzing granulated for a few seconds in a blender. Soft brown sugar is also excellent, especially for warm fruit tarts.

Salt and Pepper: For savory pastry, we like to add a pinch of sea salt and ground black pepper for extra flavor. Always use sea salt and freshly ground pepper, instead of pre-ground.

PUFF PASTRY

This rich, buttery pastry can be used for both sweet and savory tarts. Homemade puff pastry is, of course, a dream, but we recommend good-quality, ready-made puff pastry for convenience. Buy fresh or frozen, and try to buy puff pastry made with butter rather than margarine. It can be frozen for 2 months or will keep for 1 week in the fridge. Always roll out thinly, pricking the base several times with a fork, and bake in a preheated hot oven.

FILO PASTRY

Again, buy good-quality filo pastry, to use for both sweet and savory recipes, and there's no need to make your own. Fresh filo pastry can be frozen, but once it's defrosted, don't re-freeze. To use, remove the pastry from the packet and lay one sheet out on a lightly floured surface. Brush with melted butter, olive oil or beaten egg and use as directed in the recipe. Cover the pastry not in use with a damp dish towel or clean cloth. We use filo to make canapé tartlets, which are extremely versatile. Keep stored in an airtight container for up to 1 month.

FLAVOR ADDITIONS FOR SWEET PASTRY

Rosemary: Both fresh and dried rosemary are excellent in a sweet crust – try using it for an orange or lemon tart. If using fresh, finely chop the spiky leaves in a food processor before adding to the pastry ingredients.

Cocoa Powder: It's worth buying a good-quality, dark cocoa powder, such as organic, for its rich and bitter flavor. We often add sifted cocoa powder to a sweet pastry. For 8 oz pastry or one tart shell, substitute ¼ cup (1 oz) cocoa for the same amount of the flour. Try Double Chocolate Mascarpone Tart (see page 150) or a summer berry tart with a dark-chocolate pastry.

Orange and Lemon Zest: Ideal when added to a sweet pastry, especially when using summer fruits. Add about 1 teaspoon grated zest to the pastry ingredients.

Almonds, Hazelnuts, and Pecans: Ground nuts add a delicious richness to pastry. However, they do make the pastry more oily to handle, so keep the ingredients well chilled. Nuts can be roasted before using, at 350°F for 10 minutes, until golden. Cool, then grind in a food processor. We recommend ¼ cup (1 oz) of ground nuts to 1¾ cup (7 oz) flour, ½ cup (4 oz) chilled butter, 1 tablespoon sugar and 1 small egg. Always check the date on packages of nuts, as they get stale very quickly.

FLAVOR ADDITIONS FOR SAVORY PASTRY

Olives: Use rinsed and dried green or black pitted olives, and finely chop first by hand or in a food processor with the other pastry ingredients. Olives are very moist, so you'll need less egg or water to bind. Olive pastry has a lovely dark color and a distinctive flavor.

Fresh Herbs: Finely chopped basil, flat-leaf (Italian) parsley, thyme, rosemary, sage, and oregano are all great additions to savory pastry. Mix in by hand or, for better color and flavor, mix with the other ingredients in a food processor.

Parmesan cheese: Parmesan cheese is a dry cheese, so when freshly grated and added to pastry ingredients, it works extremely well. Omit salt when using Parmesan, as it's already salty.

basic pastry

● Preparation: 10 minutes   ● Cooking: 15 minutes

This recipe makes enough pastry to line a large (10-inch) tart or quiche dish or 12 individual tarts.

basic pastry

2 cups (circa 9 oz) all-purpose flour

salt and pepper

½ cup (4 oz) salted butter, chilled and diced

1 medium egg

a dash of chilled water if needed

olive pastry

Add to the Basic Pastry
1 oz chopped pitted olives or
1 tablespoon olive purée with the egg.

parmesan cheese pastry

Add to the Basic Pastry
1 oz grated Parmesan cheese with black pepper and or ¼ teaspoon cayenne pepper with the flour, first removing 1 oz of the flour.

herb pastry

If adding drier herbs such as rosemary and thyme, use
1 tablespoon

1¼ cups (6 oz) all-purpose flour

6 tablespoons (3 oz) salted butter, chilled and diced

1 large handful flat-leaf (Italian) or curly parsley (or basil or cilantro), washed and dried

salt and pepper

1 medium egg

basic pastry

1 Place the flour, a pinch each of salt and pepper, and the butter in a food processor. Process until the mixture resembles fine breadcrumbs. Add the egg and process until the pastry forms a ball. Add a dash of cold water if the egg is not binding the pastry together.

2 On a lightly floured surface, roll the pastry out thinly to line a loose-bottomed tart dish (or individual pans). Trim the tart by passing the rolling pin over the top edges. Place in the fridge for 30 minutes to rest, or freeze for 15 minutes.

3 Preheat the oven to 375°F.

4 To bake the pastry case, line it with a large piece of foil or non-stick baking parchment paper. Fill with baking beans and spread them evenly over the base. (If you do not have baking beans available, use dried chickpeas or uncooked rice).

5 Bake the pastry case for 10 minutes, then remove the paper and beans, and bake for another 5 minutes to crisp the base. Remove from the oven, and set aside until needed.

herb pastry

1 Place the flour, butter, herbs, salt, and pepper into a food processor and pulse until the parsley is well-chopped and the flour has turned green.

2 Add the egg, and pulse until the ingredients form a dough. Chill and use as required in the recipe.

filo tarts of smoked salmon, tomato, and dill with cucumber-lime salsa

● Serves: 8   ● Preparation: 45 minutes   ● Cooking: 20 minutes

Smoked salmon never seems to waver in popularity. Here it's paired with crisp filo and wrapped around crème fraîche, served with a crunchy cucumber salsa.

16 large filo pastry sheets

4 tablespoons (2 oz) butter, melted

1 lb 2 oz ripe tomatoes, deseeded, skinned and chopped

2 teaspoons oregano, chopped

salt and pepper

6 teaspoons crème fraîche

¾ lb (12 oz) smoked salmon

cucumber-lime salsa

½ cucumber

1 small handful of fresh dill

3 green onions, finely chopped

juice of 1 lime

1 tablespoon olive oil

1 For the salsa, cut the cucumber in half. Deseed by running a teaspoon down the center. Finely chop the cucumber flesh and mix with all the remaining salsa ingredients. Season to taste, cover and chill until needed.

2 Preheat the oven to 325°F.

3 Brush each filo sheet with melted butter and fold each in half. Place 2 filo sheets on top of each other at differing angles, and wedge into 8 x 4-inch shallow, loose-bottomed tart pans. Chill for 30 minutes.

4 Mix the chopped tomatoes with the oregano, salt, and pepper, and divide among the 8 tarts. Bake in the oven for 8 minutes, until the pastry is crisp and lightly browned.

5 Remove from the oven, spoon the crème fraîche on top of the tomatoes, arrange the smoked salmon on top and return to the oven for 2 minutes.

6 Pop the tarts out of the pans, and place on serving plates. Spoon a tablespoon of the salsa on top of each, or to one side.

diva**dos**

 Smoked trout can be used instead of salmon; soured cream can replace the crème fraîche; and tarragon could replace the oregano. All filo sheets vary in size, so 16 sheets is an approximate guide only.

The filo cases can be kept, unbaked, in the fridge overnight. The salsa can be made up to 6 hours beforehand, but do not add the lime juice, olive oil, salt, and pepper until 30 minutes before.

 Serve as an elegant appetizer before Grilled Swordfish or Chili-crusted Beef Fillet (see pages 97 and 60).

diva**don'ts**

Don't allow the edges of the filo tarts to burn.

roasted tomato and shallot tarte tatin

● Serves: 8　● Preparation: 1 hour　● Cooking: 30 minutes

Sweet, roasted tomatoes and shallots are nestled in a balsamic syrup on a puff pastry crust. Great for summer parties as an elegant vegetarian dish.

9 oz puff pastry

filling

20 medium Roma tomatoes, skinned (see page 22) and halved

½ cup (4 fl oz) olive oil

4 tablespoons balsamic vinegar

2 garlic cloves, finely chopped

salt and pepper

12 small shallots, peeled

2 tablespoons extra-virgin olive oil

½ cup (4 oz) sugar

4 tablespoons water

4 oz freshly grated Parmesan cheese

1　Preheat the oven to 400°F. Place the tomato halves in a shallow roasting pan, pour over the olive oil and vinegar, and sprinkle with garlic, salt, and pepper. Bake for 50 minutes and then slide off onto a large plate.

2　Roll out the puff pastry on a floured surface to fit an 11-inch shallow tart dish or cake pan (or make 8 individual tarts). Place the rolled pastry on a plate and chill for 30 minutes. Line the tart pan with non-stick baking parchment paper. (If using a heavy cake pan or tarte tatin dish, the paper is not needed.)

3　Place the shallots in a small roasting pan, sprinkle with the extra-virgin olive oil, and season with salt and pepper. Bake for 20 minutes, shaking several times to glaze.

4　Combine the sugar with the water in a saucepan and make a caramel as on page 40. Pour into the base of the prepared pan.

5　Firmly pack the tomato halves, cut side up, over the base of the prepared pan. Fill gaps with the shallots and sprinkle with Parmesan cheese. Place the rolled pastry over the filling, and tuck in the edges to fit. Prick the pastry 6 times with a fork.

6　Bake in the oven at the same temperature for 30–40 minutes, until the pastry is puffed and golden. Let the tart cool for 5 minutes before turning out. Run a knife around the edge of the tart, then invert onto a warm plate.

diva**dos**

Use plum or vine-ripened tomatoes in season; other types of tomato will be too watery.

Prepare the tart the day before. This enhances the flavors and makes it easier to turn out and then slice.

Serve with wild rocket and shaved fennel salad as a main dish.

diva**don'ts**

Don't reheat until 20 minutes before serving. Don't overcrowd the tomatoes, since this will create too much water during cooking. Divide between 2 pans if necessary. Don't leave the tomatoes in the hot pan, otherwise they will continue to cook.

filo tart with charmoula chicken

● Serves: 8   ● Preparation: 2 hours marinating plus 1 hour   ● Cooking: 30 minutes

Charmoula is a garlicky marinade from North Africa that's used to flavor just about every kind of food there. We've marinated chicken in it, before wrapping it up in crisp filo pastry and serving it with a spicy tomato jam.

circa 10–16 filo pastry sheets

6 tablespoons butter, melted

chicken filling

1 lb 10 oz boneless, skinless chicken breasts, diced

1 red onion, finely chopped

1 large carrot, finely diced

salt and pepper

1 tablespoon olive oil

½ cup (3½ oz) pine nuts, toasted

2 eggs, beaten

charmoula marinade

1 large bunch of cilantro, finely chopped

1 large bunch of flat-leaf (Italian) parsley, finely chopped

6 garlic cloves, crushed

1 tablespoon each of ground cumin, ground coriander and paprika

1 teaspoon each of saffron strands and cayenne pepper

juice of 2 lemons

4 tablespoons extra-virgin olive oil

1 teaspoon sea salt

to serve

2 x Moroccan Tomato Jam recipe (see page 27)

1 Mix the marinade ingredients together and pour over the diced chicken. Leave for at least 2 hours (or, ideally, overnight) in a cool place.

2 Sauté the onion and carrot in the oil until soft. Add the chicken, salt and pepper, and pan-fry for 5 minutes until opaque. Then drain the chicken in a large colander in order to get rid of any liquid that might make the pastry soggy. In a large bowl, combine the chicken, pine nuts, egg, salt, and pepper.

3 You can make several individual parcels or 1 large filo tart. To serve individual parcels, lay 2 pieces of buttered filo pastry on top of each other. Spoon approximately ½ cup (3½ oz) of the filling on the top of the filo, and then start to roll it up like a large spring roll, tucking the edges in as you roll. Brush with butter. Repeat the process to make 8 parcels. They should then be chilled until ready to bake.

4 To make 1 large tart, brush 6 filo sheets with butter and lay on the base of a loose-bottomed 8-inch tart pan at different angles, covering the whole base, with extra pastry hanging over the side. Place the chicken filling inside, bringing the pastry back over it at jagged angles. Brush 4 more filo sheets with butter, and crunch up on top of the pie. Chill until ready to bake.

5 Preheat the oven to 325°F. Place a flat baking sheet (or sheets) into the oven to warm.

6 Place the pie(s) on the hot sheet(s) and bake for 30 minutes. Turn the individual parcels once, then remove from the oven. If baking a large pie, take the pie out of the tart dish using potholders, and place back on the baking sheet to crisp the bottom. Bake another 10 minutes.

7 If serving hot, eat immediately with the tomato jam, or eat at room temperature, but do not reheat.

diva**dos**
Assemble the pie(s) in the morning and chill.

Excellent served with any other tomato relish or chutney.

diva**don'ts**
Don't use the very thin, papery Greek filo pastry, as it is not easy to work with.

broccoli, italian sausage, and pecorino tart with roasted cherry tomatoes

● Serves: 8   ● Preparation: 45 minutes   ● Cooking: 25 minutes

Broccoli di rapa (or purple-sprouting broccoli) is an Italian vegetable. Once blanched and pan-fried in garlic, it is deliciously crunchy and full of flavor. Here, we've combined it with Italian sausage, Pecorino chees, and oven-dried tomatoes for a tart you won't forget.

³⁄₄ lb (12 oz) all-butter puff pastry

salt and pepper

topping

circa 1 lb broccoli di rapa, or other sprouting green (16 stalks)

1 garlic clove, finely chopped

5 tablespoons olive oil

1 lb 2 oz Italian pork sausage, skins removed

1 teaspoon fennel seeds

1 teaspoon dried red chili, crushed

3 oz Pecorino cheese, grated

roasted cherry tomatoes

24 ripe cherry tomatoes, halved

2 tablespoons olive oil

1 tablespoon balsamic vinegar

garnishes

1 large ball of fresh mozzarella, ripped into pieces

1 large handful of fresh basil, torn

1 Roll out the pastry, and cut into a 12-inch circle. Alternatively, you can make 4 individual tarts that should be rolled out to 6-inch circles. Place on waxed paper and chill for 30 minutes.

2 Preheat the oven to 400°F. Place the cherry tomato halves on a baking sheet, and sprinkle with oil, vinegar, salt, and pepper. Bake for 20 minutes and remove. Increase the oven temperature to 425°F, and heat 1 or 2 large baking sheets for 15 minutes.

3 Cut the broccoli into 1-inch pieces and blanch for 2 minutes in salted boiling water. Plunge into cold water, then drain on a dish towel. Sauté the garlic in 3 tablespoons of the oil, add the broccoli, and cook for a minute, stirring. Season with salt and pepper.

4 Heat the remaining oil in a sauté pan. Add the sausage, fennel seeds, chili, salt, and pepper. Pan-fry, using a flat spoon to break the sausage into chunks, until browned.

5 Arrange the broccoli over the pastry circles, leaving a 1-inch border. Divide the sausage, Pecorino, and tomatoes into the tart(s). Fold the pastry border over the filling, pleating it as you go around.

6 Remove the baking sheet(s) from the oven and slide the tart(s) onto it/them. The heat will help the bottom pastry to crisp. Bake for 10 minutes, then lower the oven temperature to 400°F and cook for another 15 minutes, or until the pastry is golden.

7 Remove the tart(s) from the oven and immediately sprinkle on the mozzarella and basil. Serve warm.

divados

 Buy the best-quality Italian spicy garlic or herbed sausages.

The tart can be prepared in the morning and reheated in a hot oven for 10 minutes to serve.

divadon'ts

 Don't forget to put the broccoli into cold water after blanching, otherwise it will lose its brilliant green color.

diva**meats**

teriyaki beef fillet with noodles and soy dip

● Serves: 8   ● Preparation: overnight marinating and 45 minutes   ● Cooking: 15 minutes

Here's one of our favorites for Japanese style, purity, and taste.

1 x 2¼ lb beef fillet

4 tablespoons cracked black peppercorns

1 lb 2 oz Japanese green tea or soba noodles

4 tablespoons toasted sesame oil

2 tablespoons sesame seeds, toasted

24 fresh asparagus spears, trimmed

1 tablespoon light soy sauce

salt and pepper

marinade

1 cup (8 fl oz) light soy sauce

½ cup (4 fl oz) saké

4 tablespoons caster sugar

10 garlic cloves, crushed

10 green onions, chopped

1 teaspoon crushed red chili

2 teaspoons toasted sesame oil

soy dip

½ cup (4 fl oz) light soy sauce

¼ cup ((2 fl oz) rice-wine vinegar

2 tablespoons water

1 tablespoon crushed garlic

3 teaspoons sugar

1 teaspoon hot chili bean paste

2 green onions, thinly sliced

1 Mix all the marinade ingredients together and place in a plastic bag or snug container with the beef fillet for at least 2 hours or overnight.

2 Preheat the oven to 400°F. Wipe any excess marinade from the meat, and press the cracked peppercorns all over it. Sear the fillet on all sides in a hot pan.

3 Cook the noodles in salted boiling water until *al dente*. Drain well and toss with half the sesame oil and sesame seeds.

4 Char-broil or sauté the asparagus until tender and then toss with the remaining sesame oil, the soy sauce, salt and pepper.

5 Finish cooking the meat by roasting in the preheated oven for 15 minutes or until cooked to your liking – medium rare for us. Let it rest for 5 minutes before slicing thinly.

6 Place the sliced beef, garnished with asparagus, on a large platter. Swirl noodles decoratively next to it. Place guests' individual bowls of dip alongside their plates, with chopsticks to serve themselves.

diva**dos**

Order an evenly shaped beef fillet from your butcher. We advise asking to have the meat tied, as this helps it cook evenly and enhances presentation.

The meat can be served hot or cold. If serving cold, you can roast in the morning, keep in a cool place and slice just before serving. Cook the noodles the day before, drain, place in a bowl of cold water, cover and keep in the fridge. When ready to serve, drain well and dress with oil and seeds. Both sauces can be made ahead of time, making this the perfect summer party dish!

For warm serving, sear the meat in the morning and finish off the roasting in a preheated oven just before serving.

lamb fillet with roasted garlic, coriander and yogurt sauce

• Serves: 8 • Preparation: overnight marinating and 20 minutes • Cooking: 1 hour

This is a divine sauce for lamb or beef fillet. Roast garlic, coriander, and balsamic vinegar are swirled into creamy Greek yogurt. The result is outrageous!

1 x 2¼ lb lamb fillet (eye of the loin)

2 teaspoons cumin seeds, crushed

olive oil

4 garlic cloves, crushed

salt and pepper

½ lb (8 oz) young spinach leaves

a handful of fresh herbs (flat-leaf (Italian) parsley, thyme, oregano)

½ cup (3½ oz) pine nuts, toasted

sauce

2 garlic bulbs

1½ tablespoons olive oil

½ cup (4 fl oz) Greek yogurt

1 teaspoon Dijon mustard

2 tablespoons balsamic vinegar

½ teaspoon cumin seeds, toasted

1 teaspoon coriander seeds, toasted

freshly grated nutmeg

1 Rub the lamb all over with the cumin, 2 tablespoons of the oil, and garlic, cover well and leave to marinate for several hours or overnight in the fridge.

2 To make the sauce, preheat the oven to 350°F. Slice off the top quarter of the garlic bulbs to expose the cloves. Put the bulbs on pieces of aluminum foil, sprinkle with olive oil, salt and pepper, wrap up and bake for 45 minutes. Cool slightly before squeezing the garlic pulp from the skins. Purée the pulp with the rest of the sauce ingredients and some salt and pepper in a food processor. Adjust seasoning to taste.

3 Preheat the oven to 425°F. Season the lamb fillet, and sear on all sides in 2 tablespoons oil in a hot frying pan. Roast in the preheated oven for 15 minutes, or until cooked but still pink. Remove from the oven and rest for 5 minutes in a warm place.

4 To serve, pile the spinach and herbs on a large platter. Slice the lamb, arrange it over the spinach, spoon the sauce next to the lamb and sprinkle with the pine nuts.

diva**dos**

Use large, fresh garlic bulbs that don't have green sprouts.

Sear the meat in the morning and roast just before serving. Prepare the sauce in the morning and chill. Bring back to room temperature before serving.

Serve with potato cakes or Saffron-roasted Potatoes (see page 138).

diva**don'ts**

Don't use old spices – make sure they have a strong fragrance.

Don't heat the sauce or it will separate. Always serve it at room temperature.

slow-roasted tuscan pork with fennel

● Serves: 8   ● Preparation: 10 minutes   ● Cooking: about 4–5 hours

There is nothing like lusty hunks of pork that fall to pieces when you cut off the roasting strings. What's the secret? Inexpensive meat! Only leg and shoulder cuts, with their marbles of fat, can produce this result.

5 lb boneless pork shoulder or leg, tied (crackling removed)

4 garlic cloves, cut into slivers

3 tablespoons olive oil

1 tablespoon each of salt and pepper

2 tablespoons dried oregano

2 tablespoons finely chopped rosemary

1 tablespoon fennel seeds

2 teaspoons dried chili flakes

½ cup (4 fl oz) dry white wine

4 tablespoons (2 oz) butter, chilled and finely diced

to serve

lots of fresh herbs

1 Preheat the oven to 275°F.

2 Take a sharp knife and cut small slits into the meat. Insert the slivers of garlic all over the meat. Rub with 1 tablespoon of the olive oil and the salt and pepper. In a very large frying pan, sear the meat on all sides until browned.

3 Rub the remaining oil over the pork and then roll it in a mixture of the herbs and spices. Arrange on a rack in a large roasting pan. Place in the preheated low oven and cook for about 4–5 hours. The meat will be tender and fall apart when the string is removed.

4 Slice the pork and place on a platter with rosemary sprigs and other fresh herbs.

5 Spoon off any excess fat from the roasting juices and bring the juices to a boil. Add the wine, simmer for 5 minutes, and, when ready to serve, whisk in the butter. Serve hot poured over the pork.

diva**dos**

Try and get a roast that is no more than 5 inches in diameter so that it's long and thin.

Make the spice rub ahead, and store in a jar.

Serve with Celeriac and Roasted Garlic Purée, Saffron-roasted Potatoes or Gratin of Balsamic Wild Mushrooms (see pages 131, 138, and 109). Use any leftover meat to make a delectable salad or sandwiches the next day.

diva**don'ts**

Don't use pork loin – it will be too lean to cook for a long time.

Don't be tempted to cook at a higher temperature – it's the slow cooking that makes the meat so wonderfully tender.

pomegranate-marinated lamb cutlets with coriander tabbouleh

● Serves: 8   ● Preparation: overnight marinating and 1 hour   ● Cooking: 15 minutes

Please don't run when you see this long list of ingredients – it's not as bad as you think! Tart pomegranate dressing is wonderful on lamb.

3 tablespoons pomegranate molasses

1 tablespoon olive oil

2 garlic cloves, chopped

grated zest of 1 lemon

salt and pepper

24 lamb cutlets, trimmed

pomegranate dressing

⅓ cup plus 1 tablespoon (3 fl oz) olive oil

4 tablespoons pomegranate molasses

juice of ½ lemon

1 garlic clove

1 tablespoon clear honey

1 large handful (1 oz) mint

coriander tabbouleh

1½ cups (10½ oz) cracked bulgar wheat

1 teaspoon coriander seeds, toasted and ground

½ teaspoon each of cumin and fennel seeds, toasted and ground

1 red onion, finely chopped

1 teaspoon salt

½ cucumber, deseeded

4 tomatoes, deseeded

1 large handful each of flat-leaf (Italian) parsley and cilantro, finely chopped

1 small handful of mint, finely chopped

4 green onions, finely chopped

juice and grated zest of 1 lemon

cayenne pepper

4 tablespoons olive oil

1 Mix together the pomegranate molasses, olive oil, garlic, lemon zest, salt, and pepper, rub into the lamb, and leave for 2 hours or overnight.

2 For the pomegranate dressing, place all the ingredients into a food processor and purée. Taste to check the seasoning.

3 To make the tabbouleh, wash the bulgar wheat in several changes of water and drain. Place the wheat in a large bowl, cover with 1 inch of cold water, and soak for an hour. Drain the wheat, pressing down hard

to extract as much water as possible. Mix with the remaining ingredients and toss well. Taste and adjust the seasoning if necessary.

4 Grill the cutlets under a hot broiler or on a barbecue, brushing with the marinade and turning to make sure both sides are cooked and glazed properly.

5 Serve on a large platter with the tabbouleh piled high in the center, the lamb cutlets around the edge and the pomegranate dressing drizzled over the lamb.

diva**dos**

Lamb steaks can be used instead of cutlets. If pomegranate molasses is not available (it is now sold in some supermarkets, so buy a few bottles and have on hand), you can use lemon rind and juice, mixed with clear honey. Use couscous instead of bulgar wheat. Prepare according to packet directions.

Marinate the lamb and make the dressing the day before. Prepare all the ingredients for the tabbouleh the day before, but mix together with olive oil and lemon juice 2 hours before serving.

Start with the Salad Mezze Plate, or serve with Moroccan Carrots (see pages 122 and 133).

chili-crusted beef fillet with ancho and field mushroom sauce

● Serves: 8   ● Preparation: 45 minutes   ● Cooking: 20 minutes

A traditional red-wine mushroom sauce for beef fillet is boosted by an extra kick of flavor from ancho chilies. These mild, dried Mexican chilies are available at many supermarkets and have a smoky, fruity taste – great with fried polenta or mashed potatoes on a cold winter evening.

2 tablespoons mild Mexican chili powder

1 tablespoon cumin seeds, toasted and ground

1 tablespoon extra-virgin olive oil

2 ¼ lb beef fillet, trimmed of excess fat

4 tablespoons finely chopped flat-leaf (Italian) parsley

sauce

4 large ancho chilies

4 tablespoons olive oil

1 medium onion, finely chopped

4 large garlic cloves, crushed

2¼ cups (18 fl oz) dry red wine

18 oz field mushrooms, chopped

1 cup (8 fl oz) chicken stock

4 tablespoons clear honey

1 Combine the chili powder, ground cumin, and oil. Rub all over the meat and leave covered for several hours. The fillet can be cut into 8 thick steaks, or roasted whole and carved to serve.

2 To start the sauce, stem and deseed the dried chilies. Lightly toast for 30 seconds in a hot, dry saucepan. Soak in boiling water for 15 minutes, before puréeing in a food processor. Push through a sieve and set aside. You should have about ½ cup (4 fl oz).

3 Heat the olive oil in a large saucepan, add the onion and garlic and cook over low heat until soft. Increase the heat, stir in the red wine and boil until reduced by half. Add the mushrooms, stock, chili, and honey, and simmer for about 15 minutes.

4 Preheat a heavy griddle or frying pan, or preheat the oven to 400°F. Sear the beef fillet on all sides, then complete the cooking in the preheated oven for 20 minutes.

5 Allow the meat to rest before carving. Serve sliced on a bed of mushroom sauce, sprinkled with the parsley.

diva**dos**

Make the sauce the day before, and reheat before serving.

Serve with Saffron-roasted Potatoes or Asian Potato Cakes (see pages 138 and 104).

Reduce the sauce so that it is not watery. Keep it boiling until it turns glossy and thick.

diva**don'ts**

Don't purchase dry and brittle ancho chilies. They should be supple – like a piece of soft leather. Refrigerated, they will keep for at least 6 months.

mojo-marinated steaks with cilantro sauce and chilean salsa

● Serves: 8   ● Preparation: overnight marinating and 15 minutes   ● Cooking: 20 minutes

This could be the easiest dinner you have ever prepared – if you have a food processor! Mojo is a zesty, cumin-spiked marinade that's used by many cultures in South America.

2¼ lb boned beef sirloin or fillet, in one piece

mojo marinade

5 garlic cloves, finely chopped

1 teaspoon each of salt and pepper

juice of 2 oranges

2 teaspoons ground cumin

½ cup (4 fl oz) extra-virgin olive oil

cilantro sauce

2 large handfuls cilantro leaves

1 green chili, finely chopped

1 small red onion, finely diced

2 tablespoons red-wine vinegar (Cabernet Sauvignon)

½ cup (4 fl oz) extra-virgin olive oil

1 teaspoon each of salt and pepper

chilean salsa

1 medium red onion, chopped

a small handful of cilantro

9 oz cherry tomatoes (pomodorino if available)

1½ teaspoon mild sweet paprika (Spanish *pimentón*)

½ teaspoon cayenne pepper

1 teaspoon salt

½ cup (4 fl oz) extra-virgin olive oil

⅓ cup plus 1 tablespoon (3 fl oz) red-wine vinegar (Cabernet Sauvignon)

1 Combine the marinade ingredients, pour over the beef, cover, and chill overnight. Turn several times during marinating.

2 For the sauce, pulse the cilantro and chili in a food processor until roughly chopped. Place in a small bowl and add the onion, vinegar, olive oil, salt, and pepper.

3 Pulse all the Chilean salsa ingredients, except the oil and vinegar, in the food processor until they form a chunky purée. Add the vinegar and oil, pulse again, then scrape into a bowl.

4 Either barbecue the beef or sear it in a hot frying pan to brown on all sides, then roast for 20 minutes in a preheated oven at 400°F. Remove the beef, cover loosely in foil, and rest for 10 minutes.

5 Thinly slice the beef and place on a large platter with bowls of Chilean salsa and cilantro sauce next to it for guests to help themselves.

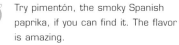

diva**dos**

Try pimentón, the smoky Spanish paprika, if you can find it. The flavor is amazing.

The cilantro sauce can be made the day before, covered and chilled. Bring back to room temperature to serve. Make the Chilean salsa several hours before serving.

The beef can be served hot or cold. Serve after Spiced Chicken Empanaditas (see page 12), and accompany with crisp potato wedges, roasted in a very hot oven with olive oil, salt, and pepper, and Tamarind-roasted Vegetables (see page 128).

diva**don'ts**

Don't slice the meat until just before serving.

meats

For those of us who are carnivores, there is nothing like the aroma of a good joint of meat being seared with black pepper or a pork roast crackling away in the oven. If your wallet can stand it, organic is the best for quality and taste. Regardless of what grade or cut is purchased, we are huge advocates of marinades, which lift the flavor of any meat. Most of our recipes use fillets, sliced steaks, and cutlets, which are not only elegant but simple for guests to eat at a party. We feel that, whenever possible, it is far better to purchase meat from a local butcher rather than supermarkets. This gives you the opportunity to ask your butcher about what you need, and will also enable you to learn more about different cuts, meats in season, quality, prices, and, often, traditional cooking methods.

BEEF

Beef Fillet: The "crème de la crème" of beef. It's so tender it doesn't require a knife, which is why it's perfect for *Diva Cooking*. We also like it because you can brown it in the morning and finish cooking in a hot oven before the meal. Beef fillet lends itself to any piquant flavors: olives, anchovies, and garlic are just a few. It is wonderful marinated in red wine, soy sauce or fresh herbs. Look for pieces that are evenly shaped so that the meat will cook to the same degree all the way through. Or ask your butcher to "string up" the fillet; this will keep the meat evenly shaped

while cooking, which is good for presentation! Try slicing the fillet 1 inch thick, then marinade in garlic, paprika, black pepper, and light soy sauce overnight. To serve, sear the steaks briefly on both sides on a hot griddle or barbecue, under a broiler, or simply in a hot, heavy-based frying pan. Try serving with Avocado-Lime Salsa (see page 17) as a light, fantastic Diva main course, or between two slices of fresh bread, with caramelized onion marmalade, crisp lettuce, Classic Mayonnaise (see page 118), and mustard to enjoy the best-ever steak sandwich!

Sirloin Steak: Like fillet, this is also an indulgent choice of meat. Sirloin is excellent for broiling and slicing thinly. Perfect for Thai Beef Salad, a Chilean-inspired steak or a teriyaki dish (see pages 126, 61 and 54), it works in any cuisine. While it's enhanced by a sharp marinade, it is equally good broiled with just salt and pepper.

Skirt Steak: The poor stepsister to sirloin, this is not only economical but full of flavor. It is a long, flat piece of meat taken from the diaphragm muscle. Marinating is advised for skirt steak, which helps to tenderize it. Any strong flavors such as garlic, soy

sauce, red-wine vinegar or herbs are perfect for the job. Once seared and sliced thinly across the grain, it is similar to more expensive grades, and is terrific grilled on the barbecue or stuffed, rolled, and roasted. It is not found regularly, but a good butcher can easily cut it for you.

LAMB

Lamb Fillet: Also known as the "eye of the loin", this extravagant cut is a special treat for lamb lovers. Used in similar dishes to beef fillet, it can adapt to any cuisine. Marinades only make it more delicious after absorbing flavors overnight. We find lamb fillet an excellent choice when catering for larger numbers. As there is little fat, once marinated, it can be seared several hours before, placed on roasting trays, and kept in a cool place until ready to be roasted in a hot oven. Carving is simple, since there are no bones to tackle. The meat is extremely tender, and therefore suits barbecues well, or can be simply grilled or broiled for smaller parties. Such a versatile meat goes just as well with the classic sauces as it does pestos, salsas, and the Middle Eastern flavors created by roasted spices, yogurts, citrus fruits, and vegetables.

Leg of Lamb: For parties, it's best to have your butcher butterfly the leg. Marinate it in something zingy such as soy sauce and copious amounts of garlic, red wine, and mint. Fresh herbs such as rosemary, thyme or oregano create a wonderful perfume when added before cooking. Excellent for serving large groups of people, it can be served with piquant sauces such as salsa verde, tomato and olive confit or mint dressing. It also works well roasted over potato gratins, or tightly covered and slowly roasted for up to 4 hours.

Lamb Cutlets: Cutlets are preferred to lamb chops as they are specifically taken from the ribcage. Chops from the neck or leg could be tougher and are not so desirable. These gorgeous little cutlets are easy to grill, love marinades and look very elegant. They work well with Mediterranean, Middle Eastern or Indian flavors. Ask your butcher to French-trim them, which means trimming all the fat off the long slender bones.

PORK

Pork Roasts: We like boneless pork roasts for parties since they're easy to prepare and look more refined than cutting the meat off the bone. Ask your butcher to bone and tie the meat for you. If you are roasting it, be sure to get the crackling fat, as you can always crisp it separately. The fat should be removed if you are braising. There are three types of roasts, which are...

Loin: The most expensive cut, it requires a higher cooking temperature and shorter roasting time. It produces firm, even slices for elegant presentation.

Shoulder: Although this is an inexpensive and tougher grade of meat, it can be sublime – try slow-roasting it on a low temperature in to create a sumptuous piece of meat. When you cut the strings off before serving, the meat falls into juicy, tender pieces.

Leg: Exactly the same principles apply to the leg roast as the shoulder. It offers terrific value for money and an impressive result.

All pork roasts work fabulously with vinegar, garlic, herb, and olive oil marinades. Try some balsamic vinegar, rosemary or thyme and olive oil to marinate the meat before roasting. Dry spices and herbs such as fennel seeds, oregano, and chili powder are excellent when rubbed over the roast while cooking. Always make sure that the roast is not sitting directly in the pan by propping it up with a rack. It's imperative that pork should always be cooked until it is no longer pink. Use a meat thermometer to gauge the internal temperature of 176°F, and make sure you don't overcook or dry the meat out.

butterflied leg of lamb with slow-roasted tomato, basil, and olive confit

- Serves: 8 ● Preparation: overnight marinating and 45 minutes
- Cooking: 3½ hours and 35 minutes

Soy sauce, wine, garlic, and mint are the most exquisite marinade ingredients for any red meat. After slow-roasting or broiling, it becomes even more delicious with tomato confit. This is a great plan-ahead dish for large groups.

1 x 4–lb leg of lamb, butterflied

marinade

¾ cup (6 fl oz) red wine

⅓ cup plus 1 tablespoon (3 fl oz) light soy sauce

3 garlic cloves, chopped or crushed

1 small handful fresh mint, chopped, plus extra for garnishing

confit

12 plum tomatoes, halved

2 garlic cloves, thinly sliced

⅞ cup (7 fl oz) olive oil

½ cup (2 oz) black olives, pitted and chopped

12 basil leaves, torn, plus extra for garnishing

salt and pepper

1 Preheat the oven to 225°F. To make the confit, place the tomato halves on a roasting tray with a slice of garlic on each. Drizzle with some of the olive oil, season with salt and pepper, and roast for 3½ hours. Remove from the oven, cool, and dice the tomatoes into large chunks. Mix with the olives and basil, and stir in the remaining oil. Set aside.

2 To prepare the meat, remove any unwanted fat using a sharp knife, but leave some on for flavor. Flatten it by placing the meat on a work surface, fat side down. Make long cuts, one in the center and one on each outside flap. Cover with a piece of waxed paper and pound with a rolling pin until evenly flat. Place in a large bowl.

3 Mix together the marinade ingredients and pour over the meat. Marinate for 4 hours or overnight.

4 Preheat a barbecue or broiler. When hot, remove the lamb from the marinade and pat dry with paper towels. Cook for 40 minutes, or until pink, turning several times. Allow to rest for 10 minutes before carving.

5 Place slices of the meat on a warm platter, serve with the confit, and garnish with lots of extra herbs.

diva**dos**

Ask your butcher to butterfly the lamb for you.

The marinade can be made days before, covered and chilled, as can the confit (store in a screw-top jar and keep cool).

The lamb is best marinated 24 hours ahead. Turn over several times during marinating.

Excellent in the summer, or try in winter with Saffron or Red Pepper Aïoli (see pages 73 and 85). Serve with Fennel Slaw, Saffron-roasted Potatoes or Baby Green Salad (see pages 134, 138 and 135).

diva**don'ts**

Don't use dark soy sauce since it is too salty.

gingered beef with honey and prunes

● Serves: 8   ● Preparation: 30 minutes   ● Cooking: 2 hours

Despite their dowdy reputation, prunes are a brilliant ingredient to cook with. Adding a subtle sweetness, they are ideal for spicy Moroccan tagines and stews.

2¼ lb chuck or braising steak, sliced

all-purpose flour

salt and pepper

olive oil

3 onions, finely chopped

2 garlic cloves, chopped

4-inch piece of fresh root ginger, grated

3 teaspoons ground cumin

1¼ cups (10 fl oz) each of red wine and meat stock

2 tablespoons clear honey

¾ lb (12 oz) ready-to-eat stoned prunes

1 tablespoon pomegranate molasses

relish

1 red onion, finely sliced

1 small handful of fresh flat-leaf (Italian) parsley, chopped

seeds of 1 pomegranate (optional)

1 tablespoon olive oil

½ tablespoon red-wine vinegar

1 Cut the beef slices into 3-inch pieces, put in a bag and shake in the flour, salt, and pepper. Heat 2 tablespoons of olive oil in a large casserole, and sear the meat on all sides. Remove, and add a little more oil. Fry the onions, garlic, and ginger for 10 minutes on a medium to high heat, then add the cumin and cook for another 2 minutes.

2 Return the meat to the pan, add the red wine, stock, and honey, and bring to a boil. Add the prunes, cover, and simmer for 1½ hours.

3 The meat should be tender and easy to cut. Add the pomegranate molasses and cook for another 30 minutes, part of the time covered.

4 To make the relish, mix all the ingredients together and season to taste.

5 Serve the beef in a warm dish, with the relish spooned on top.

diva**dos**

Make this casserole 1 or 2 days ahead, as the texture, color, and flavor will benefit enormously. If you are short on time, garnish with parsley or cilantro instead of relish.

Be sure to simmer the meat over a very low heat, and keep it covered during cooking.

Start with the Spicy Shrimp or Salad Mezze Plate (see pages 27 and 122), and serve with Celeriac and Roasted Garlic Purée (see page 131).

diva**don'ts**

Don't allow your butcher to dice the chuck steak as normal – make sure you buy sliced steak. Don't despair if you can't find pomegranates – the relish does work without it.

roast fillet of beef with cilantro and peanut pesto

● Serves: 8 ● Preparation: 4 hours marinating and 20 minutes ● Cooking: 25 minutes

This superbly elegant dish is ideal for a summer fusion menu. It has serious flavor as well!

2¼ lb beef fillet, in one piece

1 tablespoon olive oil

marinade

2 red chilies, deseeded

2 garlic cloves, peeled

1 tablespoon clear honey

4 tablespoons olive oil

2 tablespoons each of dark and light soy sauce

juice of 2 limes

cilantro and peanut pesto

4½ oz unsalted peanuts

1 bunch of green onions, washed and dried

½ lb (8 oz) fresh cilantro

2 green chilies, deseeded

1-inch piece fresh root ginger, chopped

1 garlic clove, chopped

1 tablespoon rice-wine vinegar

juice of ½ lemon

1 tablespoon teriyaki sauce

2 tablespoons sesame oil

salt and pepper

1 To make the pesto, purée all the ingredients in a food processor. Check the seasoning, cover, and chill.

2 Trim the fillet of any excess fat with a sharp knife. Purée all the marinade ingredients in a food processor, then pour over the fillet. Marinate for 4 hours.

3 Preheat the oven to 400°F.

4 Remove the beef from the marinade and pat dry. Heat the oil in heavy-based frying pan and sear the beef well on all sides. Remove from the pan, place in a large roasting pan, and roast for 25 minutes in the preheated oven. Test with a sharp knife. Allow the meat to rest for 10 minutes before carving.

5 Carve the meat in ½-inch slices. Place on a warm serving platter with bowls of the cilantro-peanut pesto.

diva**dos**

Sirloin steak can replace fillet.

The cilantro and peanut pesto can be made the day before.

The beef can be served hot or cold. Serve with Caramelized New Potatoes or Baby Green Salad (see pages 136 and 135). Garnish with strips of green onion, chili, cilantro leaves or toasted sesame seeds.

diva**don'ts**

Don't hesitate to remove the meat from the oven before it is cooked to your liking, as it will continue to "cook" while resting.

divabirds

braised duck legs with soy sauce, ginger, and star anise

- Serves: 8 • Preparation: 15 minutes • Cooking: 1½ hours

Duck is forever glamorous. This is an excellent make-ahead party dish that will fill your home with fragrant aromas.

8 duck legs

4 tablespoons honey

1 teaspoon Chinese five-spice powder

5 garlic cloves, sliced

2½-inch piece fresh root ginger, cut into strips

1 cup (8 fl oz) chicken stock

5 tablespoon saké

½ cup (4 fl oz) red wine

½ cup (4 fl oz) light soy sauce

4 star anise

garnish

½ bunch of green onions, julienned

2 red chilies, deseeded and julienned

1 Preheat the oven to 350°F.

2 Trim excess fat from under the duck legs. Brown the legs in a hot frying pan with no oil. Place in a large roasting tray, drizzle with the honey, and sprinkle with the five-spice powder.

3 Tip out any duck fat from the frying pan, then add the garlic and ginger and sauté for 2 minutes. Add all the liquids and the star anise, bring to a boil and simmer for 5 minutes.

4 Pour the ginger liquid around the duck and seal tightly with foil, ensuring there are no holes. Roast in the preheated oven for an hour. Remove the foil and increase the oven temperature to 425°F. Cook another 15 minutes to crisp the skin (or place under a hot broiler).

5 To serve, place the duck legs on a warm platter. Discard any fat and spoon the remaining juices around the duck. Garnish with the green onions and chili.

diva**dos**

 Some duck legs are juicier than others; we use Gressingham.

The duck can be cooked well ahead of time and kept covered with foil. To reheat, place into the oven at 350°F for 15 minutes, remove the foil, and cook for another 15 minutes. If the juices start to dry up, add some boiling water, bring to a boil, and whisk to combine the juices.

 We serve with a chicory, watercress, red onion, and pear salad, lightly tossed in lemon juice and olive oil.

diva**don'ts**
Be careful not to burn the juices when crisping the duck.

guinea fowl breasts with tarragon and crème fraîche

● Serves: 8 ● Preparation: 15 minutes ● Cooking: 30 minutes

A French classic that has been given a revamp: seared, tender guinea fowl in a creamy, tart sauce, enlivened with fresh tarragon.

8 guinea fowl breasts

2 tablespoons (1 oz) butter

1 teaspoon each of salt and pepper

20 large shallots, roughly sliced

1 cup (8 fl oz) tarragon vinegar

½ cup (4 fl oz) white wine

½ cup (4 fl oz) chicken stock

2 bunches of fresh tarragon, stems removed, leaves chopped

½ cup (4 fl oz) crème fraîche

1 Melt the butter in a large, deep saucepan and brown the guinea fowl on both sides. Sprinkle with salt and pepper, and remove from the pan.

2 Sauté the shallots in the same pan until soft and golden. Add the vinegar and boil to reduce by half.

3 Place the guinea fowl back in the saucepan. Add the wine, stock, and half the chopped tarragon. Cook,

uncovered, over a low heat for 20–30 minutes, or until the guinea fowl is tender. Add the crème fraîche and remaining tarragon just before serving.

4 Serve with long-grain white rice.

diva**dos**

Ask your butcher to bone the guinea fowl, but to leave a decorative wing bone. You can use other poultry, such as chicken thighs and breasts.

This recipe freezes well and can be made a day ahead to reheat at 325°F.

Start the evening off with Sun-blush Tomato Pesto with Pita Breadsticks (see page 11), and serve with Baby Green Salad with Classic Vinaigrette (see pages 135 and 118).

diva**don'ts**

Don't let the dish boil once the crème fraîche has been added or it may separate.

korean barbecued chicken with cucumber salad

● Serves: 8   ● Preparation: 2 hours marinating plus 30 minutes   ● Cooking: 15 minutes

Korean food is relatively unfamiliar. Sweet, sour, and spicy, lots of garlic and sesame oil are the quintessential flavors. Here, marinated grilled chicken is wrapped in crunchy lettuce and served with a spicy cucumber salad.

16 boneless, skinless chicken thighs

16 lettuce leaves (iceberg or romaine)

marinade

8 tablespoons Korean sweet-spicy chili paste (kochujang)

¾ cup (6 fl oz) saké or mirin

3 tablespoons light soy sauce

3 tablespoons crushed garlic

3 tablespoons sesame salt

4 tablespoons sesame oil

3 tablespoons grated fresh root ginger

2 tablespoons pepper

1 tablespoon salt

6 green onions, finely sliced

cucumber salad

2 small cucumbers, deseeded (if large, then use 1)

4 tablespoons rice-wine vinegar

1 teaspoon each of salt and pepper

1 tablespoon sugar

1 teaspoon dried crushed red chili

1 Mix all the marinade ingredients together. Pour over the chicken and leave refrigerated for at least 2 hours, but preferably for a day or overnight.

2 For the salad, thinly slice the cucumbers. Mix the remaining ingredients and pour over, cover, and refrigerate for at least half an hour before serving the chicken.

3 Place the chicken under a hot, pre-heated broiler or on a barbecue, for about 10 minutes each side, or until cooked.

4 Serve the chicken on a platter with the lettuce on the side. Guests can bundle their chicken in the lettuce and top with the cucumber salad before wrapping.

diva**dos**

Look for kochujang in a Japanese or Asian food store, or try one of the new internet sites for ethnic foods. Substitute another chili paste if you cannot get it.

Marinate the chicken the night before – this saves time on the day of the party.

Serve the chicken on a large white platter decorated with more green onion or cilantro leaves. Simplicity is best for Asian food. Serve with other Asian favorites like Thai Green Papaya Salad with Seared Chili Shrimp or Tamarind-roasted Vegetables (see pages 120 and 128).

brochettes of lemon chicken, sage, and croûtons with red-pepper aïoli

- Serves: 8   • Preparation: 30 minutes marinating plus 1 hour   • Cooking: 15 minutes

A wondrous combination of flavors and textures from Tuscany, perfect for a summer picnic. You will need 16 wooden skewers, which you should soak in water for an hour beforehand.

6 boneless, skinless chicken breasts

12 slices of prosciutto, each cut into 4 strips

½ stick of French bread

32 sage leaves

3 garlic cloves, finely chopped

juice and grated zest of 1 large, juicy lemon

salt and pepper

4 tablespoons olive oil

red-pepper aïoli

1 red pepper, quartered and deseeded

1 cup (8 fl oz) Classic Mayonnaise (see page 118)

3 garlic cloves

juice of 1 lemon

1 small handful of fresh basil

1 To make the aïoli, place the pepper quarters under a very hot broiler, skin side up, and grill until the skin has blackened. Remove and place in a bag to cool. Peel the pepper, discarding the skin. Place with all the remaining aïoli ingredients in a food processor and purée until smooth. Adjust seasoning to taste. Keep chilled until ready to serve.

2 Cut the chicken into 48 equal chunks. Wrap each chunk in a slice of prosciutto.

3 Cut the bread into 32 equal-sized chunks. Onto each skewer, thread a piece of chicken, a sage leaf,

a chunk of bread, followed by chicken, then sage and bread, finishing with a piece of chicken. Repeat this process for all 16 skewers.

4 Mix together the garlic, lemon juice, zest, salt, and pepper with the olive oil, and brush liberally over the brochettes. Leave to marinate for 30 minutes.

5 Preheat a large frying pan, broiler, or barbecue. Sear the chicken for 15 minutes, turning 2 or 3 times. Serve with the aïoli.

divados

 Chicken thighs can be used instead. You can substitute rosemary skewers for plain wooden ones (see page 20).

The brochettes can be assembled the day before, covered, and chilled. Marinate them up to an hour beforehand. The aïoli can be made 2 days before, covered and chilled.

 Arrange the chicken on a large serving platter, with sprigs of herbs and a large bowl of the aïoli. Serve with Saffron-roasted Potatoes or Fennel Slaw (see pages 138 and 134).

divadon'ts

Don't use stainless-steel cutlery when making or serving the aïoli, or it will take on a metallic flavor. Use wooden or silver spoons.

seared duck breasts with balsamic vinegar, rosemary, and shallot sauce

● Serves: 8   ● Preparation: 1 hour marinating plus 15 minutes   ● Cooking: 30 minutes

We made this years ago at the Books for Cooks Valentine's Day dinner. It was such a success that we had to include it in the book!

8 duck breasts

marinade

1 tablespoon clear honey

2 tablespoons light soy sauce

salt and pepper

balsamic, rosemary, and shallot sauce

1 tablespoon olive oil

6 shallots, finely sliced

2 tablespoons chopped rosemary

½ cup (4 fl oz) red wine

1 cup (8 fl oz) balsamic vinegar

¾ cup (6 fl oz) chicken stock

1–2 tablespoons fruit jelly, such as crab-apple or elderberry

4 tablespoons (2 oz) butter, chilled and diced

1 Preheat the oven to 375°F.

2 Trim any excess fat from the duck breasts. Mix together the marinade ingredients, pour over the duck and leave for 1 hour.

3 Heat a heavy frying pan, add the duck and brown well on both sides. Remove from the pan, place in a roasting tray and roast in the preheated oven for 10–15 minutes until still pink. Allow to rest for 5 minutes before carving.

4 To make the sauce, heat the olive oil in a saucepan. Wilt the shallots and rosemary, cooking until caramelized, about 10 minutes. Add the wine and balsamic vinegar, bring to a boil and reduce to an eighth. Add the stock and reduce by half. Whisk in the fruit jelly, simmer for 5 minutes, then bring back to a boil. Whisk in the chilled butter to thicken and enrich the sauce.

5 Serve the duck sliced on warm plates with the sauce.

diva**dos**

We use Gressingham duck breasts. Do not use cheap balsamic vinegar, as it will affect the taste of the sauce. Redcurrant jelly works well but does have quite a strong flavor.

Marinate the duck the day before. The sauce can be made earlier in the day, but do not add the butter until reheating to serve.

We serve it with Mashed Sweet Potato and Ginger (see page 130), a roasted pumpkin purée or string beans tossed in toasted sesame seeds and light soy sauce.

You can sear the duck hours before, then roast in the hot oven at the last minute. Allow to rest for 10 minutes.

balsamic chicken with porcini mushrooms and sun-dried cherries

● Serves: 8   ● Preparation: 30 minutes   ● Cooking: 45 minutes

This elegant braised chicken is the perfect make-ahead meal. Porcini mushrooms, balsamic vinegar, and dried cherries are a divine combination. Serve with any mashed vegetable for a great winter meal.

about ½ cup (2 oz) dried porcini mushrooms

8 large boneless, skinless chicken thighs

4 tablespoons all-purpose flour

1 teaspoon each of salt and pepper

½ lb (8 oz) pancetta bacon, diced, or smoked bacon, chopped

1 tablespoon olive oil

2 onions, finely chopped

6 garlic cloves, finely chopped

20 dried cherries, roughly chopped

½ cup (4 fl oz) balsamic vinegar

2¼ cups (18 fl oz) red wine

½ cup (8 fl oz) chicken stock

1 teaspoon arrowroot or cornstarch, dissolved in 2 teaspoons cold water

a handful of flat-leaf (Italian) parsley, chopped

1 Pour 1 cup (8 fl oz) boiling water over the porcini mushrooms. Leave for half an hour, then carefully strain through a fine sieve, reserving the liquid. Roughly chop the porcini.

2 Dredge the chicken in seasoned flour and set aside. Fry the pancetta in a little olive oil until it is very crisp. Remove from the pan and set aside. Brown the chicken pieces on both sides in the bacon fat. Remove from the pan, then sauté the onions and garlic until soft.

3 Stir the porcini mushrooms into the onion along with the cherries, vinegar, red wine, stock, and reserved porcini liquid. Bring to a boil and simmer for 10 minutes.

4 Add the chicken and pancetta, bring to a simmer, and cook for 30 minutes. Add the arrowroot or cornstarch mixture and simmer for another 5 minutes. Check the seasoning and adjust with additional salt or balsamic vinegar.

diva**dos**

Make this dish the night before to save time and improve the intensity of flavors.

Serve with any type of white mashed vegetable or vegetable purée. Celeriac, potatoes, or Jerusalem artichokes are all yummy possibilities. Start with Spiedini of Scallops or Grilled Red Peppers (see pages 87 and 106).

diva**don'ts**

Don't use poor-quality balsamic vinegar – splurge on superior brands like Fini, if available.

birds

Poultry is probably the most widely eaten meat in the world. Because of its mild flavors, it can be enhanced with zesty marinades and sauces, or simply paired with fresh herbs. On a hot, summer day there is nothing like the taste of barbecued chicken with crispy skin. Duck is the favorite for more formal events, turkey is for holidays, and chicken for ethnic and casual meals. We recommend organic, corn-fed or free-range chickens for their superior taste and texture.

DUCK

Duck Legs: These are best-known for their role in the classic French confit. Not only are duck legs inexpensive, but the meat is tender and flaky when braised. Asian flavors such as soy sauce, garlic, chilies, ginger, and green onion are excellent baked with legs. Mediterranean ingredients such as balsamic vinegar, thyme, prunes, and olives are also fantastic additions. As duck can be fatty, cut off excess fat and sear the portions, skin side down, to render the fat. The liquid fat can then be drained off before braising. For large duck pieces, buy Barbary duck legs, and for smaller portions, purchase Gressingham.

Duck Breasts: The most prized part of duck, breasts are perfect for an elegant occasion. Purchase the smaller Gressingham birds, which are lean and full of flavor, or female Barbary, which are far smaller than the male ducks. Because the fat is so thick on the breasts, trim off any overlapping fat and, using a sharp knife, score the skin in a diamond pattern to let the fat flow out when searing. Marinating the breasts before cooking helps keep them juicy. Port, red wine, balsamic vinegar, soy sauce, honey, and pomegranate molasses are just a few of the flavors that combine best with duck breasts. You can also include spices such as juniper berries, roasted cumin seeds, and star anise. To cook, preheat a heavy, dry frying pan, sear the duck for several minutes on both sides, then place in a hot oven and roast for 10 minutes until pink. Allow the meat to rest for 5 minutes in a warm place before slicing. Duck breasts can also be grilled or barbecued.

Wild Duck: Wild duck is a real game-lover's treat. It's available from your butcher or game dealer from early September until late January to mid-February. The most common varieties are teal, mallard, and widgeon – but which to choose? Well, here's a quick guide: the mallard (a relation of the farmyard duck) is an omnivorous bird, so we would recommend the widgeon, which feeds only on grass, and is famed for its excellent flavor. The tiny teal is also a little gem, especially if there aren't many mouths to feed! Make sure you reserve the carcass to make a deliciously rich, gamey stock, which will enhance any winter sauce beyond your expectations!

To make the most of your wild duck breast, we recommend marinating it overnight with crushed juniper berries, a little honey, and some port. The wild duck can then be seared and roasted by following the same methods employed in other duck recipes (see pages 38, 68 and 74). Try serving the breast with our Balsamic Vinegar, Rosemary and Shallot Sauce (see page 74), or any other sauce that you would normally serve with duck.

To make the duck stock (this method works equally well with all game birds), begin by placing the carcass in a large stockpot with a couple of chopped onions, carrots, mushrooms, bay leaves, 6 black peppercorns, and a parsley stalk. Cover and bring to a boil, then reduce the heat immediately, and simmer for two hours, regularly skimming the stock. Next, strain the stock and discard the carcass and all other ingredients. Pour the liquid into a clean pan and reduce by half over a high heat – this will create a fuller, more concentrated, more satisfying flavor! Cool the stock and decant – you can then either chill in the fridge for two days before use, or freeze. Wild duck stores extremely well, and like all poultry, it can be frozen for up to six months, so it can be enjoyed out of season. When freezing, ensure that the meat is well-wrapped and labeled to avoid confusion or damaging the texture or flavors.

CHICKEN

Chicken Thighs: We think boneless chicken thighs are the best-kept secret in town. They're far cheaper than breasts, juicier, and great value for money. Be sure and cut off any excess fat before cooking. Boneless chicken thighs are fantastic for skewering, barbecues, stews, and pan-frying. Almost any flavor can be used with them: Moroccan, Southeast Asian, Middle Eastern, Mediterranean, or Japanese. They are superb if marinated before cooking in anything from garlic and olive oil to Korean sweet spicy chili paste or kochujang (see page 71).

Chicken Breasts: Chicken breast meat can be pan-fried or broiled for a casual gathering, as well as grilled, stuffed, and sliced for lavish dinners. Careful thought must be given to how chicken breasts are cooked to keep them nice and juicy – they can become rubbery and dry. Marinating in vinaigrettes, yogurts, coconut milk, Asian sauces, or citrus-fruit juice is highly recommended. They are best served with very gutsy sauces such as salsa verde, sweet chili sauce, spicy chili salsas, or charmoula. Poaching chicken breast works well – cool the chicken in the poaching water, then shred or slice chicken to use.

Guinea Fowl: This bird is very similar to chicken but darker in color and with a slightly gamier taste. Guinea fowl is becoming increasingly popular. It is well-suited to French Provençal flavors such as tarragon, crème fraîche, bacon, thyme, olives, and garlic. With a tendency to dryness, guinea fowl needs careful cooking and should be basted frequently, or prepared with a sauce to prevent drying out. "Supremes", which are a breast cut with the wing bone attached at the top, are especially good for parties. Ask your butcher to prepare them for you. The wing bone serves no other purpose than looking elegant. (You could also remove the bones and use them to make an excellent stock.)

Poussin: These are four- to six-week-old baby chickens, and they are absolutely lovely to barbecue and grill. They are best prepared by a process known as "spatchcocking", which is removing the backbone, flattening, and securing with metal skewers. This helps the tiny birds cook evenly and quickly. They benefit from marinating overnight to help keep the flesh moist. Thai, Chinese, and Mediterranean marinades all produce delicious results. A poussin generally serves one person, but if including with other dishes as part of a meal, allow half a bird per head.

grilled indonesian coconut chicken

● Serves: 8   ● Preparation: 4 hours marinating plus 20 minutes   ● Cooking: 20 minutes

The Indonesians have a genius for marinating with big flavors. The aroma of the lemongrass, ginger, and garlic will drive your guests crazy. This recipe is excellent for summer, when barbecuing is at its height.

16 boneless, skinless chicken thighs

cilantro leaves

marinade

4 lemongrass stalks, outer leaves discarded, root ends trimmed

a large handful of cilantro, chopped

6 shallots, sliced

8 large garlic cloves

fresh root ginger, chopped

4 tablespoons brown sugar

2 tablespoons curry powder

2 teaspoons pepper

½ teaspoon salt

4 tablespoons Thai fish sauce (nam pla)

1¾ cups (14 fl oz) coconut milk

1 Finely chop the lower 6 inches of the lemongrass stalks, discarding the remainder, then slice. In a food processor or blender, finely grind together the lemongrass, cilantro, shallots, garlic, and ginger. Add the sugar, curry powder, pepper, salt, fish sauce, and coconut milk, and blend to a purée.

2 Place the chicken in a suitable container. Pour the marinade over the chicken, covering well. Chill overnight, or for at least 4 hours. Remember to turn once or twice.

3 Preheat a broiler or barbecue, or set the oven to its highest temperature.

4 Grill or roast the chicken in its marinade for 20 minutes, turning over once to caramelize. Serve on a large platter sprinkled with cilantro leaves.

diva**dos**

Cut excess fat off the chicken thighs as well as the skin.

Marinate 24 hours ahead for perfect flavor and time saved on the day.

 We suggest serving with white rice, but as part of an Asian menu, serve with Thai Beef Salad and Green Papaya Salad with Seared Chili Shrimp (see pages 126 and 120).

diva**don'ts**

Don't overcook, as the chicken will quickly dry out.

smoky chipotle chicken with pineapple salsa

● Serves: 8 ● Preparation: 1 hour ● Cooking: 15 minutes

Discovering chipotle chilies is one of life's greatest treats. They impart a spicy, smoky flavor to any dish, but use them sparingly, since they are powerfully hot.

8 large, boneless, skinless chicken thighs, trimmed of all fat, or 6 boneless, skinless chicken breasts

2 tablespoons peanut oil

7–8 ripe plum tomatoes, halved

8 garlic cloves, unpeeled

2–3 chipotle chilies in adobo sauce, or dried chilies, rehydrated in water (stemmed and deseeded)

a small handful of cilantro

salt and pepper

1 large onion, chopped

3 tablespoons vegetable oil

grilled pineapple salsa

2 tablespoons vegetable oil

1 fresh pineapple, peeled and cut into slices

juice of 3 limes

1 large red onion, chopped

1 large handful cilantro, chopped

to serve

16 flour tortillas

crème fraîche

cilantro leaves

1 Pan-fry the chicken thighs slowly in the oil until they are browned and cooked through. Chop or shred while hot.

2 Broil the tomatoes until black on both sides. Place the garlic in a non-stick saucepan, and blacken both sides over a medium heat. Cool and peel. Roughly purée the tomatoes, garlic, chipotles, the cilantro, salt, and pepper in a food processor.

3 Sauté the chopped onion in the oil in a saucepan. Add the shredded chicken and stir-fry for 10 minutes. Pour on the tomato paste and cook to thicken for about 5 minutes.

4 Preheat a broiler or barbecue. Brush oil on the pineapple slices and grill on both sides until black lines appear. Remove and cut out the round core in each piece. Roughly chop the pineapple and combine with the remaining salsa ingredients and some salt and pepper.

5 Prepare the wraps by heaping 4 tablespoons of the warm chicken into the center of each tortilla. Top with 2 tablespoons pineapple salsa and 1 teaspoon crème fraîche. Fold the bottom of the tortilla up about 1-inch and fold the sides over. Leave the top open and sprinkle with cilantro leaves. Serve immediately.

diva**dos**

Buy a can of chipotle chilies in adobo sauce, found at specialty markets or by mail order, and keep covered in an airtight container. They will last for at least 6 months.

Cook the shredded chicken the day before and chill. Prepare the salsa on the morning of the party.

 Serve on a platter decorated with grilled lime halves and loads of cilantro. Start the evening off with Spiced Corn Cakes or Tuna Ceviche (see pages 17 and 32) and their respective salsas.

diva**don'ts**

Don't use green pineapples – look for firm ones with a golden color.

seared thai chicken with tomato-chili jam

● Serves: 8   ● Preparation: 1 hour marinating plus 25 minutes   ● Cooking: 45 minutes

Simply marinated chicken paired with a sweet and piquant chili jam. It's possibly one of our all-time favorites.

8 boneless, skinless chicken breasts

marinade

4 tablespoons sesame oil

4 tablespoons Thai fish sauce (nam pla)

1 tablespoon clear honey

3 garlic cloves, chopped

2 red chilies, deseeded and finely chopped

1 large handful of cilantro, finely chopped

tomato-chili jam

1¼ lb ripe tomatoes, chopped

4 red chilies, deseeded and chopped

4 garlic cloves

1 x 2–inch piece of fresh root ginger, chopped

2 tablespoons Thai fish sauce (nam pla)

1¼ cups (10 oz) soft brown sugar

½ cup (4 fl oz) red-wine vinegar

3 Thai lime leaves

2 oz raisins

1 To make the tomato-chili jam, place half the tomatoes, the chili, garlic, ginger, and fish sauce in a food processor and blend to a purée. Place this purée in a heavy-based saucepan with the sugar, vinegar, lime leaves, and raisins, and bring to a boil slowly, stirring. Chop the remaining tomatoes into small cubes and add to the jam once it has come to a boil. Simmer gently for 45 minutes, stirring occasionally. If the tomatoes are very watery, it may need longer, but the jam will thicken when cold.

2 Slice the chicken into thick strips. Mix the marinade ingredients together, pour over the chicken, cover, and chill for 1 hour or up to 1 day.

3 Preheat a large frying pan, broiler or barbecue. Sear the chicken for 5 minutes on each side, brushing with the marinade as it cooks.

4 Serve hot or cold. If serving hot, keep warm in a medium oven until ready to eat. Pile onto a large serving plate alongside bowls of chili jam.

divados

Use chicken thighs instead. If time is short, bottled Thai sweet chili sauce is an excellent substitute for the jam.

Make the jam a month ahead and keep chilled in a screw-top jar. The chicken can be marinated the day before the event.

We often serve this chicken on wooden skewers, which makes great party fare. It is best cooked to serve, but you can cook 30 minutes before and keep warm in a medium oven. Serve with large lime wedges and cilantro, and we sometimes sprinkle it with toasted sesame seeds. Mashed Sweet Potatoes and Ginger, Fragrant Coconut Rice or Tamarind-roasted Vegetables (see pages 130, 139 and 128) are the ideal accompaniments to this dish.

divafish

grilled shrimp with tamarind recado and pineapple and red onion salsa

- Serves: 8 • Preparation: 30 minutes marinating and 1 hour • Cooking: 5 minutes

Shrimp taste fabulous marinated and basted with recado, a spicy, sweet-and-sour Mexican marinade. Here the recado is prepared with gorgeous tamarind, which makes a lovely glaze.

40 large raw shrimp, peeled

tamarind recado

½ cup (4 oz) tamarind pulp (in a sticky block) or 1¼ cups (10 fl oz) bottled tamarind purée

1½ cups (12 fl oz) boiling water

10 garlic cloves, unpeeled

1 onion, thickly sliced

4 plum tomatoes, halved

3 dried chipotle chilies, in adobe sauce, or 3 dried chilies, rehydrated in water (stemmed and deseeded)

1 tablespoon salt

2 tablespoons brown sugar

salsa

18 oz coarsely chopped fresh pineapple

1 red onion, finely chopped

a large handful of cilantro, chopped

juice of 2 limes

salt and pepper

1 To make the recado, place the tamarind pulp in a bowl and pour in the boiling water. Leave to soak until soft and fairly liquid. Press through a sieve and set aside. (Or use the bottled tamarind purée instead). Place the garlic in a hot, dry frying pan and cook over a high heat until softened and charred. Cool, then peel. Preheat a broiler, place the onions and tomatoes underneath until blackened.

2 Place the tamarind liquid, chilies, onion, tomatoes, garlic, salt, and sugar in a food processor and blend until smooth.

3 In a shallow dish, coat the shrimp with the recado, cover, and leave to marinate in the fridge for 30 minutes to 1 hour. Soak bamboo skewers in water for at least 30 minutes.

4 Mix the salsa ingredients together and season to taste.

5 Thread the shrimp onto the skewers and grill or barbecue for 5 minutes, basting with the remaining marinade during cooking. Serve with the salsa.

divados

Buy tamarind pulp from an Indian or Thai food store. Larger city supermarkets may have bottled tamarind.

The recado can be made up to 12 days ahead. Make the salsa on the day of serving.

The shrimp look fantastic served on banana leaves, garnished with cilantro sprigs and lime wedges.

divadon'ts

Don't buy popcorn shrimp. Get jumbo-size – they will be worth it.

Don't overcook the shrimp, as they will become tough and rubbery.

spicy crab cakes with cherry tomato and cilantro salsa

● Makes: 16   ● Preparation: 45 minutes   ● Cooking: 20 minutes

These crispy crab cakes work well served as an appetizer or main course, or they can be made canapé-size to serve a crowd.

crab cakes

¾ lb (12 oz) white crabmeat, well-drained, if canned

1 red onion, finely chopped

2 tablespoons honey

1 teaspoon crushed dried red chilies

about 4 cups (8 oz) fresh breadcrumbs

1 cup (8 fl oz) Classic Mayonnaise (see page 118)

1 egg

1 large handful cilantro, finely chopped

salt and cayenne pepper

grated zest and juice of 2 limes

1 teaspoon Tabasco sauce

½ cup (4 fl oz) sunflower or peanut oil

cherry tomato and cilantro salsa

4 green onions, finely chopped

1 small handful cilantro, chopped

½ lb (8 oz) ripe cherry tomatoes, quartered

2 red chilies, deseeded and finely chopped

1 tablespoon Thai fish sauce

juice of 1 lime

the garnish

baby salad leaves or rocket leaves

lime wedges

1 Place all the crab-cake ingredients, except the oil, in a large bowl and mix together. Shape the mixture into 16 even-sized cakes and chill.

2 To make the salsa, mix all the ingredients together and season to taste.

3 Heat a little of the oil in a large, heavy-based frying pan. Cook the crab cakes in batches over a medium heat for about 2 minutes on each side, turning them over once. Add extra oil as needed. Keep the crab cakes warm in a moderate oven.

4 Serve on a bed of salad leaves, garnished with lime wedges and little bowls of the salsa.

diva**dos**

Use canned white crab or fresh crabmeat.

The crab cakes can be made the day before serving and kept chilled in the fridge. Make the salsa up to 6 hours ahead, but do not add the seasoning, fish sauce or lime juice until 30 minutes before serving.

The crab cakes can be fried 1 hour before serving and kept warm in a moderate oven.

Serve as an appetizer before Roast Fillet of Beef with Cilantro and Peanut Pesto or as a main course with Parsley and Roasted Garlic Tart and Fennel Slaw (see pages 66, 38 and 134). Crème fraîche is also delicious with the crab cakes.

fennel and seafood bouillabaisse with saffron aïoli

● Serves: 8 ● Preparation: 50 minutes ● Cooking: 30 minutes

An extremely elegant soup, perfect for a special occasion.

soup

2 tablespoons olive oil

3 garlic cloves, finely chopped

2 onions, finely chopped

1 fennel bulb, finely chopped

2 carrots, finely chopped

1 potato, peeled and chopped

½ cup (4 fl oz) dry white wine

3 ¾ cups (30 fl oz) fish stock

3 tomatoes, deseeded and chopped

juice of 1 lemon

salt and cayenne pepper

1 ¼ lb monkfish tail, skinned and sliced into thick pieces

8 king scallops, trimmed

16 raw jumbo shrimp, peeled

chopped fresh dill to garnish

saffron aïoli

2 pinches of saffron threads

2 tablespoons boiling water

2 egg yolks

3 garlic cloves, finely chopped

juice of 1 lemon

1 teaspoon Dijon mustard

½ teaspoon sugar

1 ¼ cups (10 fl oz) sunflower oil

1 To make the aïoli, place the saffron in a small bowl, pour in the water and leave for 5 minutes. Place the egg yolks, garlic, lemon juice, mustard, and sugar in a food processor. Slowly drizzle in the oil and blend to form a thick, creamy mayonnaise. Add the saffron liquid, season to taste, then chill.

2 For the soup, heat the olive oil in a large saucepan, add the garlic and vegetables, and cook gently for 5 minutes, until softened. Add the wine, then the stock and tomatoes. Bring to a boil, then reduce the heat, cover, and simmer for 20 minutes. Add lemon juice and seasoning.

3 Just before serving, add the fish to the simmering soup and cook gently for 5 minutes, until just tender. The shrimp will turn pink. Serve in warmed bowls, sprinkled with dill. Pass the aïoli in a bowl separately for guests to spoon onto their soup.

diva**dos**

Alternative fish may be added, such as cod, baby squid or lobster.

This is an excellent party dish, as the aïoli and the vegetable broth can be made well ahead.

Add the fish to the broth just before serving, to keep it tender.

Serve as an elegant starter or hearty main course, with the vegetables and fish cut into larger chunks. Serve with Miniature Focaccia or Diva Breadsticks (see pages 161 and 158).

spiedini of scallops with a chunky salsa verde

● Serves: 8   ● Preparation: 25 minutes   ● Cooking: 10 minutes

Once you experience salsa verde, you can become seriously addicted to it!
Not only is it packed with flavor, it's healthy and simple to make. We've updated
it slightly with crunchy red onion for more texture. Delicate scallops make the
perfect partner. Allow 3 scallops as an appetizer or 4 for a main course.

8 x 10-inch rosemary sprigs

24–32 large scallops, shelled

2 tablespoons olive oil

juice of 1 lemon

salsa verde

1 large bunch of flat-leaf
(Italian) parsley

1 bunch of basil leaves

10–15 mint leaves

2 garlic cloves, peeled

2 anchovies, rinsed

2 tablespoons capers, rinsed

3 tablespoons red wine vinegar

1 teaspoon mustard

salt and pepper

¾ cup (6 fl oz) extra-virgin olive oil

1 small red onion, finely diced

1 Take the rosemary sprigs and pull
off most of the needles, leaving just
those at the top, to make herb
skewers. Sprinkle the scallops with
olive oil, salt, and pepper. Thread
3–4 scallops onto each rosemary
sprig. Chill until ready to cook.

2 Place all the ingredients for the
salsa verde in a food processor,
except the olive oil and red onion.

Pulse until the mixture is roughly
chopped. Slowly add the oil until it
is all incorporated. Scrape into a
bowl and add the red onion.

3 Preheat a heavy sauté pan.
Add the scallop skewers in batches
and sear for 1 minute on each side.
Squeeze over the lemon juice. Serve
on a large platter and accompany
with the salsa verde.

diva**dos**

Leave the orange muscle on the
side of the scallops – it's very tasty.
Raid your neighbors' gardens for
large sprigs of rosemary – the
supermarket variety won't be long
or strong enough.

You can make the salsa verde
the day before. Keep it covered and
chilled. Thread the scallops
on the rosemary skewers on
the morning of the party.

If cooking for a large number,
sear the scallops quickly in advance
and allow to cool. Later, preheat
the oven to 400°F. Just before
serving, roast the scallops in the
oven for 5 minutes.

Serve with Grilled Red Peppers
stuffed with Herbed Ricotta or
Tuscan Panzanella Salad (see pages
106 and 123) for the ultimate
Mediterranean feast.

diva**don'ts**

Don't overcook the scallops, as
they will shrink and lose their
precious juices.

shrimp dumplings in fragrant thai broth

- Serves: 8 regular servings or 6 greedy ones
- Preparation: 30 minutes
- Cooking: 30 minutes

Delicate shrimp dumplings in a tasty coconut broth make this a meal in itself. The ingenious ingredient, tom yum paste – which is the Thai equivalent of stock cubes – provides a wonderful sweet, spicy, and sour flavor.

shrimp dumplings

1 garlic clove, peeled

1-inch piece of fresh root ginger

2 shallots, peeled

½ lb (8 oz) raw shrimp, peeled

1 egg white

1 teaspoon cornstarch

2 tablespoons chopped fresh cilantro

salt and pepper

stock

shrimp shells and heads (optional)

2 chunks of fresh root ginger, peeled and chopped

6 garlic cloves, sliced

a large handful of cilantro stalks, chopped

coconut broth

1³⁄₄ cups (14 oz) coconut milk

½ cup (4 oz) tom yum paste

4 lime leaves, finely chopped

2 tablespoons Thai fish sauce (nam pla)

juice of 2 limes

about 1 cup (4 oz) fresh shiitake mushrooms, thinly sliced

¼ lb (4 oz) baby corn, sliced in half lengthwise

a small handful of basil leaves, torn

cilantro leaves to garnish

1 To make the dumplings, place the garlic, ginger, and shallots in a food processor, and pulse until finely chopped. Add the shrimp, egg white, cornstarch, cilantro, and seasoning. Purée to a rough paste. Chill until needed.

2 For the stock, heat 3½ quarts of water in a large saucepan or stockpot. Add the shrimp shells and heads, if using, the ginger, garlic, and cilantro stalks. Bring to a boil, then reduce the heat and simmer for 20 minutes. Sieve and discard the solids.

3 Pour the stock back into the pan and add the coconut milk, tom yum paste, lime leaves, fish sauce, and lime juice. Bring back to a boil, then simmer for 5 minutes. Season to taste.

4 Five minutes before serving, add the mushrooms and baby corn to the soup.

5 Using a teaspoon, shape the shrimp mixture into little balls and drop into the simmering soup. Cook for 3–4 minutes until they float to the top. Add the basil.

6 Ladle into bowls and garnish with cilantro leaves.

diva**dos**

Buy tom yum paste from a Thai food store or large city supermarket. Once opened, it will keep well in the fridge. If unavailable, replace with 2 fish or tom yum stock cubes. Do buy unpeeled shrimp – the shells really enhance the flavor of the stock.

You can prepare the soup and the dumpling mixture the day before serving.

Serve the soup in Asian ceramic bowls – very Diva! Serve with Thai Green Papaya Salad with Seared Chili Shrimp or Soba Noodle Salad (see pages 120 and 119).

sweet potato, shrimp, and ginger fritters with cucumber relish

● Makes: 16   ● Preparation: 20 minutes   ● Cooking: 15 minutes

Crunchy fritters with succulent shrimp, topped off with a refreshing cucumber relish. Yum!

fritters

¾ cup (3 oz) all-purpose flour

3 medium eggs, separated

1 teaspoon salt

a large pinch of cayenne pepper

1¾ lb (14 oz) sweet potato, grated

3 green onions, finely chopped

1-inch piece of fresh root ginger, peeled and grated

1 small handful cilantro, finely chopped

16 raw jumbo shrimp, peeled

4 tablespoons peanut oil

cucumber relish

½ cup (4 fl oz) rice-wine vinegar

2 tablespoons caster sugar

1 carrot, finely chopped

2 shallots, finely chopped

1-inch piece of cucumber, deseeded and finely chopped

1 red chili, deseeded and finely chopped (or ½ teaspoon crushed dried red chili)

1 small handful cilantro, chopped

grated zest and juice of 1 lime

1 Place the flour, egg yolks, ½ cup (4 fl oz) cold water, salt and cayenne pepper in a bowl and mix to a smooth paste. Stir in the sweet potato, green onions, ginger and cilantro. Whisk the egg whites until stiff, then fold into the mixture to make a batter.

2 Slice the shrimp in half lengthwise. Heat 4 tablespoons of the oil in a non-stick frying pan. Take 1 tablespoon of the fritter batter and add 2 shrimp halves. Slide the fritter into the hot oil and fry for 2 minutes on each side, until golden and crispy. Repeat with the remaining mixture and shrimp, adding more oil if needed. Keep the fritters warm until ready to serve.

3 To make the relish, gently heat the vinegar and sugar in a saucepan until the sugar has dissolved. Bring to a boil, then boil for a few minutes until syrupy. Remove from the heat, allow to cool, then add the remaining relish ingredients. Adjust the seasoning if necessary. Serve with the fritters.

diva**dos**

If tight for time, you could use bottled Thai chili dip to serve in place of the relish.

The relish vegetables can be chopped and chilled the day before, but the relish should be finished on the day of serving. Add more chili if you like spicy food. The batter for the fritters can be made (without adding the egg whites) up to 2 hours before serving and kept chilled. Add the beaten egg whites just before frying.

The fritters can be cooked up to 30 minutes before serving, then kept warm.

Serve the fritters hot on a large white platter, garnished with cilantro sprigs and lime wedges, with the relish in small dipping bowls. Serve the fritters with Korean Barbecue Chicken or Vietnamese Chopped Chicken Salad (see pages 71 and 115).

fish

Fish is not only quick to prepare, it's also light, tasty, and healthy. Fish doesn't need elaborate techniques or sauces; it's delicious served simply. When shopping, look for fresh-smelling fish with bright eyes and a firm body with shiny skin and clean gills. Purchase on the day, or the day before, you plan to serve. For parties, we don't advise serving anything with bones or shells in it. It is important to mention the global issue of vastly declining fish stocks and seriously damaged ecosystems that are a growing concern among seafood consumers and the fishing industry – ask your supermarket or local environmental group for guidance about purchasing ecologically safe seafood.

SEAFOOD

Shrimp: BUY BIG! Small shrimp for a glamorous party look stingy, so get the jumbo size. Look for shrimp in the shell that have no black spots, and always smell them to check for freshness. Oriental supermarkets are a great place to buy frozen shrimp, as they import excellent quality for a fair price. When preparing, peel off the shells, leave on the tail and butterfly both sides, removing the veins. Shrimp should not marinate for longer than 1 hour. They are best barbecued on skewers, grilled or pan-fried. They take just a few minutes to cook, so remove them from the heat as soon as they turn opaque.

Scallops: These little treasures are sweet, tender and terribly glamorous. If cost is not a consideration, scallops are impressive and easy to prepare. The smaller size are called "queen" and work well as a canapé. For starters and main courses, use the large "king scallop". With their delicate flavor, scallops are perfect with piquant sauces such as salsa verde (see page 87) or sweet chili sauce. Do not remove the delicious pink coral – it is the tastiest part. Slice off the small white muscle found on the side of each scallop. Good scallops, if purchased really fresh, will keep in the fridge for 2 days before preparing. Searing and grilling are the best methods of cooking scallops. They only

need 30 seconds to 1 minute for each side, otherwise they will overcook and shrink, losing their precious juices. For large parties, you can prepare scallops ahead of time. Briefly sear them on both sides in a hot pan, then immediately cool and chill. Then, just before serving, roast them in a hot oven for about 4 minutes.

Crab: For most *Diva* recipes, buying crabs already dressed is recommended. If you do buy fresh whole ones, look for crabs that are heavy, with the claws drawn tightly into the body. Use a hammer to break the body and crackers to open the legs. Discard the back part with the legs and any dubious-looking pieces. We

only like using the white meat to cook with. The brown meat is stronger and not suitable for most prepared dishes. Crab is best known for its star role in crab cakes. Breadcrumbs and other ingredients can make a little meat go a long way. It is also delicious in Thai salads, tarts, pastas and canapés.

SMOKED FISH

Smoked Salmon: Top-quality smoked salmon is readily available in vacuum-sealed packs. We like to use it for sophisticated canapés, served on toast cut into stars, mini-blinis, cucumber cups, or filo tartlets. It's also great in potato and summer pasta salads and pairs beautifully with capers, dill, crème fraîche, roasted peppers, and red onions.

Smoked Trout: With its bright-pink color, smoked trout looks dazzling and is used like smoked salmon. It contrasts well with pumpernickel, toasted and cut into shapes with horseradish. Crème fraîche, yogurt, red chilies, cilantro, and citrus-fruit sauces all marry well with it.

MEDITERRANEAN AND ROUND FISH

Monkfish: Monkfish is very popular due to its lack of bones and meaty texture. Because it's thick and sturdy, it can be poached, seared, roasted or barbecued without falling apart. Look for monkfish that are firm, fresh-smelling, and that have the fine purple membrane removed – and buy on the day of preparation or the day before. Mediterranean ingredients partner it best: olives, tomatoes, anchovies, capers, and saffron. Monkfish is wonderful in the classic soup known as Bouillabaisse (see page 85).

Cod: Another member of the round fish family, cod was once relegated in England almost exclusively to fish and chips. As its scarcity continues, cod is slowly becoming an exclusive fish. Prized for its flaky, white meat and light texture, it can be used with many flavors. It is delicious baked with potatoes, herbs and cream, and is equally superb steamed with Thai herbs, baked, and drizzled with saffron aïoli or prepared with an exotic miso paste glaze. Look for thick, firm pieces of fish that have not been frozen.

Sea Bass: Its flaky, white flesh is excellent poached, grilled, pan-fried, or baked, with a soft and delicate flavor. Look for firm, thick, fresh-smelling steaks or fillets. Works well with citrus-fruit vinaigrettes, herb sauces or garlic-roasted vegetables.

Halibut: Its firm, white flesh may be an expensive delicacy, but it is sublime poached, braised or baked with white wine, cream, herbs, and lemon. Try to find firm, thick steaks or fillets.

LARGE FISH

Tuna: There are many varieties of tuna: albacore, skipjack, yellowfin, and bluefin. Most are canned, except the exclusive bluefin – its prized red flesh is sold for sushi or fillet steaks. High-quality fresh tuna is fabulous eaten raw, if consumed on the day of purchase, as sashimi, in a Latin ceviche, or diced for Asian tartare. The texture is meat-like, so it stands up well to marinating and grilling. Strong ethnic flavors such as Moroccan, Japanese, Sicilian, Thai, or Mediterranean are best. It should be cooked rare, so sear it quickly on each side. It's wonderful in salads. To keep the flesh tight, buy a thin loin and roll in crushed peppercorns. Sear all over, then rest until cool. Wrap tightly in plastic wrap and refrigerate overnight. Slice the next day.

Swordfish: Swordfish can be prepared similarly to fresh tuna. It's sold in steaks. In the markets of Palermo, you can see fishermen cutting off whole slices from a 4-foot fish. Look for light-pink steaks with little fat marbling. Swordfish absorbs marinades well. Strong flavors such as vinegars, charmoula, anchovies, lemon, and garlic are wonderful partners. Lightly grill or pan-fry and serve with zesty salsas or vinaigrettes.

miso glazed cod

● Serves: 8   ● Preparation: 24 hours marinating and 10 minutes   ● Cooking: 10 minutes

This is adapted from Nobu restaurant's signature dish. Of course, they never give out their recipes, but through chatting to friendly waiters, a lot of tenacity, and careful testing, we think we've come pretty close.

8 x 6-oz cod fillets (skin on)

the marinade

½ cup (4 fl oz) saké, Chinese rice wine or dry sherry

½ cup (4 fl oz) mirin

½ cup (4 fl oz) miso paste

2 tablespoons light soy sauce

3 tablespoons brown sugar

4 tablespoons chopped green onions to garnish

1 Place the fish in a shallow glass dish. Mix together the ingredients for the marinade, pour over the fish to coat thoroughly, then cover. Refrigerate for a minimum of 24 hours or up to 3 days (the fish is perfectly preserved with the salty miso).

2 Preheat a hot broiler. Remove the fish from the marinade and place on a baking sheet, skin side down. broil for 10 minutes, without turning, until cooked through. Serve immediately, sprinkled with the green onions.

diva**dos**

Do venture into a Japanese grocery store to stock up on miso paste, mirin, and saké.

Try and allow 2–3 days for the fish to marinate. It makes a big difference to the flavor.

Grill the fish just before your guests are ready to eat.

Serve on its own with elegant lemon halves covered in yellow muslin, tied with ribbon – perfect for minimalists! Or serve with a selection of accompaniments, such as Tamarind-roasted Vegetables and Fragrant Coconut Rice (see pages 128 and 139).

diva**don'ts**

Don't buy cod that has been previously frozen. Fresh cod is very important in this recipe.

monkfish, bacon, and dill pie with mashed potato, green onions and parmesan

• Serves: 8   Preparation: 35 minutes   • Cooking: 25 minutes

A classic favorite made slightly more upmarket.

filling

4 tablespoons (2 oz) butter

1 onion, finely chopped

³/₄ lb (6 oz) rindless bacon, diced

1¹/₄ lb monkfish fillet, skinned and cut into chunks

2 leeks, thickly sliced

¹/₄ cup (1 oz) flour

1³/₄ cups (14 fl oz) milk

2 tablespoons (1 fl oz) cream

4 teaspoon wholegrain mustard

a large handful of fresh dill, chopped

grated zest of ¹/₂ lemon

a pinch of nutmeg

salt and pepper

the topping

1 lb 10 oz potatoes, boiled and mashed

2 tablespoons (1 fl oz) cream

2 tablespoons (1 oz) butter

4 green onions, finely chopped

2 oz Parmesan cheese, grated

1 Preheat the oven to 350°F. Heat half the butter in a large, non-stick frying pan. Add the onion and bacon, and sauté gently for 5 minutes. Add the fish and sauté until just sealed.

2 Blanch the leeks in boiling water for 5 minutes. Drain well.

3 Gently melt the remaining butter in a saucepan, stir in the flour, and cook for 1 minute. Remove the pan from the heat and gradually add the milk and cream. Return to a low heat and bring to a boil, whisking continuously. Add mustard, dill, lemon zest, nutmeg, and seasoning.

4 Gently fold the fish mixture and leeks into the sauce, then spoon into a large ovenproof serving dish.

5 Mix the warm mashed potatoes with the cream, butter, green onions, and Parmesan cheese. Season to taste. Pile the mashed potatoes on top of the fish and bake for 25 minutes, until golden and crispy.

diva**dos**

Any of your favorite fish, such as shrimp, cod or smoked haddock, can be added to this versatile pie.

This dish is excellent for winter parties, since it can be prepared ahead and freezes well.

Cut the monkfish into medium-sized chunks (no smaller), to keep them from breaking up.

Start the evening off with Golden Shallot Pancakes with Tapenade (see page 10). For added glamour, make the pies in individual pots and garnish with chopped chives. Serve with a crispy salad of chicory, watercress, and red onion.

seared tuna with couscous and sicilian vinaigrette

● Serves: 4   ● Preparation: up to 1 hour marinating and 20 minutes   ● Cooking: 5 minutes

Sicilian cuisine is fascinating because of its strong roots in both North African and Italian ingredients. You won't find couscous in any other part of Italy. The capers and anchovies are the stars here, making everything burst with flavor.

1 pint (16 fl oz) couscous

a pinch of saffron powder or threads

½ cup (4 fl oz) boiling chicken stock

4 fresh tuna steaks

cilantro leaves to garnish

sicilian vinaigrette

2 tablespoons capers, finely chopped

1 anchovy, rinsed and finely chopped

1 garlic clove, finely chopped

1 teaspoon crushed dried chilies

15 mint leaves, chopped

1 small handful of fresh cilantro, chopped

a small handful of flat-leaf (Italian) parsley, chopped

¼ cup (2 fl oz) red-wine vinegar

½ cup (4 fl oz) extra-virgin olive oil

salt and pepper

1 Place the couscous in a bowl. Add the saffron to the chicken stock, pour over the couscous, and mix until coated. Spread it thinly up the sides of the bowl and leave to dry for 5 minutes.

2 Place the capers, anchovy, garlic, chilies, and herbs in a screw-top jar. Add the vinegar and oil, screw on the lid tightly, and shake well. Season to taste.

3 Pour ⅓ of the vinaigrette over the tuna steaks in a shallow dish. Leave to marinate for at least 5 minutes but ideally for 1 hour.

4 Just before serving, preheat a hot grill or barbecue. Crumble the couscous into fine grains, then reheat in a steamer or microwave.

5 Grill or barbecue the tuna for 5 minutes, turning halfway through the cooking, until tender. Pile the couscous on a large plate, lay the tuna on top, and garnish with cilantro leaves. Pour the remaining vinaigrette over the fish and couscous, and serve immediately.

diva**dos**

Look for tuna steaks that are bright-red in color with little fat. Swordfish steaks could also be used instead of tuna.

Get ahead and prepare the couscous and vinaigrette the day before the event.

Some lemon halves make an attractive garnish. Serve with Tuscan Panzanella Salad (see page 123).

diva**don'ts**

Don't overcook tuna. It's best eaten medium-rare.

seared scallops and monkfish on curried red lentils with yogurt sauce

● Serves: 8   ● Preparation: 30 minutes   ● Cooking: 50 minutes

Red lentils cooked with fragrant spices and a refreshing yogurt sauce provide the perfect backdrop for delicate-tasting fish.

1 lb 9 oz monkfish fillet, skinned

6 slices prosciutto

16 large scallops, trimmed

juice of ½ lemon

2 tablespoons olive oil

salt and pepper

lentils

1 tablespoon olive oil

1 onion, finely chopped

2 garlic cloves, chopped

1-inch piece of fresh root ginger, peeled and grated

1 teaspoon ground cumin

1 teaspoon curry powder

½ lb (8 oz) split red lentils

2½ cups (20 fl oz) chicken stock

juice of ½ lemon

1 tablespoon Greek yogurt

yogurt sauce

1 cup (8 fl oz) Greek yogurt

1 small handful fresh mint, chopped

1 green chili, deseeded and finely chopped

garnish

finely shredded green onions

cilantro leaves

lemon wedges

1 Cut the monkfish into 16 even-sized chunks. Cut each slice of prosciutto into 3 and wrap a piece around each chunk of monkfish, including the little left over. Place the scallops in a small bowl and toss with the lemon juice, 1 tablespoon of the olive oil, and seasoning.

2 To prepare the lentils, heat the olive oil in a large pan, add the onion, garlic, ginger, cumin, and curry powder, and sauté gently, stirring, for 3–4 minutes. Add the lentils and stir to coat for 2 minutes.

3 Add the stock, bring to a boil, then reduce the heat, cover, and simmer for 45 minutes, or until the lentils are soft. Add the lemon juice, yogurt, and seasoning.

4 For the sauce, mix the yogurt, mint, and chili in a serving bowl.

5 Heat the remaining olive oil in a large non-stick frying pan. In batches, sear the scallops and monkfish parcels for 5 minutes or until cooked through. Drain off any liquid that weeps from the fish. Keep the cooked fish warm in a low oven.

6 To serve, spoon the warm curried lentils onto a platter, pile the fish on top and garnish with green onions, cilantro leaves and lemon wedges. Serve with the yogurt sauce.

divados

We used scallops and monkfish, but you could use cod fillets and shrimp or chunks of chicken breast tossed with crushed garlic, lemon juice, and olive oil.

The spiced lentils can be made a day ahead, then reheated over a low heat. A little extra chicken stock/water may be needed. The fish can be prepared for cooking the day before and kept covered in the fridge.

To avoid overcooking the fish in a last-minute rush, sear it in a hot pan earlier in the day, then place on a roasting tray and chill. Just before serving, roast the fish in a hot oven for 5–8 minutes.

Start the evening off with Indian Pakoras (see page 30) and serve with a light green salad. Scoop up the sauce with our Cumin Flatbread (see page 163).

grilled swordfish with rosemary, tomato, and caramelized onions

● Serves: 8   ● Preparation: 1 hour marinating and 10 minutes   ● cooking: 1 hour

This recipe was inspired by a recipe from Tra Vigne, a restaurant in California's Napa Valley. It's quite Sicilian with its flavors of lemon zest, caramelized onions, and sweet tomatoes, and makes a delightful main course.

8 swordfish fillets, about (5½ oz) each

marinade

juice and zest of 2 lemons

4 tablespoons olive oil

1 tablespoon chopped rosemary

salt and pepper

sauce

5 tablespoon olive oil

5 onions, thinly sliced

2 tablespoons chopped rosemary leaves

3 x 14 oz cans peeled plum tomatoes

4 tablespoons red-wine vinegar

2 oz raisins, chopped

grated zest of 2 lemons

juice of 1 lemon

2 tablespoons sugar

4 tablespoons chopped flat-leaf (Italian) parsley, to garnish

1 Combine the ingredients for the marinade in a shallow dish. Add the fish and leave for at least 1 hour, covered and chilled.

2 To make the sauce, heat the olive oil in a saucepan and add the onions with the rosemary and seasoning. Cook gently for 20 minutes, stirring occasionally, until the onions start to caramelize.

3 When the onions are golden, add the tomatoes, vinegar, raisins, lemon zest, lemon juice, and sugar. Cook for 30 minutes or until the mixture is thick. Season to taste.

4 Preheat a hot broiler. Remove the fish from the marinade and grill for about 3 minutes on each side, depending on the thickness of the steaks – they may take a little longer.

5 To serve, pour the warm sauce into a large, deep platter, place the fish on top and sprinkle with the chopped parsley.

diva**dos**

Do splurge on swordfish or other firm-fleshed fish, like sea bass or halibut. It's also worth spending a little more on good-quality canned tomatoes for this dish.

You can make the sauce the day before. Keep it chilled.

Start your meal with Marinated Fig, Glazed Shallot and Prosciutto Salad or Tuscan Panzanella Salad (see pages 125 and 123). Follow with the fish.

diva**don'ts**

Don't cook the fish until your guests are ready to eat.

diva**veggies**

tomato bruschetta with asparagus, gorgonzola, and basil salad

- Serves: 8 regular servings or 6 greedy ones • Preparation: 25 minutes

Our friend Rita lives in California and she is a regular shopper at the weekly farmers' market. She says that the ingredients are so superb that she now only arranges food instead of cooking it! This dish is not far off that concept and does require outstanding tomatoes.

topping

40 thin asparagus spears

1 teaspoon baking soda

1¼ lb cherry tomatoes
(preferably pomodorino)

2 garlic cloves, finely chopped

4 shallots, finely chopped

4 tablespoons extra-virgin olive oil

juice of 2 lemons

grated zest of 1 lemon

1 large bunch of fresh basil,
thinly sliced

salt and pepper

½ lb (8 oz) Gorgonzola or dolcelatte
cheese, crumbled

basil leaves to garnish

toasts

8 large slices of sourdough or French
country bread, sliced at an angle

6 tablespoons extra-virgin olive oil

1 whole garlic clove, peeled

1 Trim the tough stalks from the asparagus, saving only the tender part of the stalks and the tips. Bring a large pan of lightly salted water to a boil. Add the baking soda, then drop in the asparagus and blanch for 1 minute. Drain and immediately refresh in cold ice water to preserve the bright-green color – otherwise, asparagus can turn an unappealing grey.

2 Slice the cherry tomatoes in half and mix together with the garlic, shallots, olive oil, lemon juice and zest, basil, salt, and pepper.

diva**dos**

Buy the tomatoes a few days early and allow them to ripen in a bowl at room temperature. Please don't ever refrigerate tomatoes, as it damages their flavor. Sourdough bread has a chewy texture that's perfect for bruschetta; a white country bread would also be fine.

3 Preheat the oven to 400°F. Brush the bread with the olive oil, and toast in the oven for about 4 minutes. Rub each bruschetta with the raw garlic clove. (If preferred, the toasts can be made under a hot broiler.)

4 Drain the asparagus and pat dry with paper towels. Place 5 asparagus spears on each slice of bread. Pour the tomato mixture over, dividing it equally between the bruschetta, and scatter the crumbled cheese over the top. Serve immediately, garnished with basil leaves.

Serve with any of the Diva tarts or barbecue dishes for a perfect summer party.

diva**don'ts**

Do not assemble the bruschetta until just before serving.

polenta-crusted eggplant with roasted tomatoes, buffalo mozzarella, and salsa verde dressing

- Serves: 8   - Preparation: 30 minutes salting and draining eggplants and 15 minutes
- Cooking: 1 hour

Let's face it: what doesn't taste good fried and served with salsa verde? Here, eggplant is made extra crispy with a coating of polenta, then served with roasted plum tomatoes, creamy mozzarella, and the wonderful herb sauce.

6 ripe plum tomatoes, halved

2 tablespoons extra-virgin olive oil

1 tablespoon balsamic vinegar

salt and pepper

2 large eggplant, sliced into ½-inch rounds

3 medium eggs

1 cup (8 oz) polenta or fine cornmeal

1¾ pint (28 fl oz) sunflower oil, for frying

2 buffalo mozzarella cheeses, each torn into 6 pieces

salsa verde dressing

1 large handful flat-leaf (Italian) parsley

1 large handful basil

1 tablespoon capers, washed and drained

2 garlic cloves, peeled

1 tablespoon red-wine vinegar

½ cup (4 fl oz) extra-virgin olive oil

1 Preheat the oven to 300°F. Lay the tomatoes on a baking sheet, drizzle with olive oil and balsamic vinegar, and season with salt and pepper. Roast for 1 hour.

2 Lay the eggplant slices on a large tray, sprinkle with salt, and leave for 30 minutes. Whisk the eggs together in one bowl and place the polenta in another.

3 Heat the sunflower oil in a deep, heavy-based saucepan. Rinse the eggplant slices and dry with paper towels. Dip the slices first in the egg, then in the polenta, coating thoroughly. Carefully fry in the hot oil,

in small batches, until crisp and golden. Drain on paper towels.

4 Place all the ingredients for the salsa verde dressing in a food processor and purée until smooth. Season to taste.

5 To serve, arrange the hot eggplant slices around the edge of a large platter or individual serving plates. Place the roasted tomatoes in the center, and scatter the mozzarella pieces over the top. Spoon over the salsa verde or serve it separately in a bowl.

diva**dos**

Salsa verde can be made with other green herbs such as cilantro or mint.

The salsa verde can be made a day ahead and kept covered and chilled. The tomatoes can also be roasted a day ahead.

Do dry the eggplants well after rinsing. The slices can be coated with egg and polenta 30 minutes before frying. Once fried, they can be kept warm for 30 minutes.

Serve as an appetizer or with Brochettes of Lemon Chicken, Sage and Croutons with Red Pepper Aïoli or Slow-roasted Tuscan Pork with Fennel (see pages 73 and 57).

roasted winter vegetables in a fragrant coconut sauce

● Serves: 8   ● Preparation: 30 minutes   ● Cooking: about 35 minutes

A colorful selection of root vegetables are roasted until sweet, then finished off with a delicately spiced coconut sauce. This is delicious with steamed basmati rice and a piquant chutney for a vegetarian main dish.

vegetables

1 lb 9 oz sweet potatoes, peeled and cut into 1-inch cubes

1 eggplant, cut into 1-inch cubes

3 red onions, quartered

2 red peppers, deseeded and cut into 1-inch pieces

16 fresh baby corn

⅓ cup plus 1 tablespoon (3 fl oz) extra-virgin olive oil

salt and pepper

coconut sauce

5 tablespoon sunflower oil

2 large onions, finely chopped

10 garlic cloves, finely chopped

2 x 2-inch pieces of fresh root ginger, grated

2 tablespoons ground coriander

2 tablespoons ground cumin

1 teaspoon salt

2 teaspoons turmeric

4 plum tomatoes, skinned and diced

1¾ pint (28 fl oz) coconut milk

1 pint (16 fl oz) vegetable or chicken stock

1 small handful fresh cilantro, chopped

20 mint leaves, chopped

1 Preheat the oven to 400°F. Place all the vegetables in a large roasting pan, then drizzle with the olive oil and season with salt and pepper. Roast in the preheated oven for 20 to 30 minutes, or until the vegetables are golden. Remove from the oven and set aside.

2 For the sauce, heat the oil in a large saucepan, add the onions and sauté for 5 minutes, then add the garlic and ginger. Cook for 3 minutes, stirring frequently, then add the spices and cook, stirring for 2 minutes.

3 Add the tomatoes, coconut milk, and stock, and simmer for 15 minutes.

4 Add the roasted vegetables to the sauce and then simmer for 5 minutes. Just before serving, add the chopped cilantro and mint.

diva**dos**

You can complete this entire dish up to 2 days ahead, then keep chilled until required.

To reheat, warm gently in a covered pan or dish in a moderate oven. Do not stir too much, as you don't want to break up the vegetables.

Serve with Fragrant Coconut Rice (see page 139) and a delicious tomato or mango chutney.

smoky black-bean tacos with cherry tomato salsa

● Serves: 8   ● Preparation: 30 minutes plus overnight soaking   ● Cooking: 1 hour

This delectable black-bean purée can be used as a dip or filling or made into bean cakes. If we were vegetarians, this is what we would live on! Cider vinegar, cumin, and honey are the big flavors that give the beans a huge boost. Mix up some margaritas or sangria and have a fiesta.

1¼ lb dried black beans, soaked overnight

6 tablespoon extra-virgin olive oil

2 onions, chopped

2 red peppers, chopped

2 chipotle chilies in adobo sauce, or 2 dried chipotles, rehydrated in water (stemmed and deseeded)

8 garlic cloves, chopped

2 teaspoons sea salt

½ cup (4 fl oz) cider vinegar

½ cup (4 fl oz) honey

2 teaspoons chili powder

2 teaspoons ground cumin

16 corn tortillas

1¼ pints corn oil, for frying

the salsa

1¼ lb cherry tomatoes, halved

1 red onion, chopped

1 small bunch of cilantro, chopped

juice of 2 limes

salt and pepper

crème fraîche or sour cream to serve

1 Drain the soaked beans. Cover with fresh water in a medium saucepan, bring to a boil, and simmer for 1 hour, or until they are just tender.

2 Heat the olive oil in sauté pan. Add the onions, peppers, chilies, garlic, and salt. Sauté for 5 minutes, then add the beans. Stir in the vinegar, honey, chili powder, and cumin. Simmer over a low heat for about 5 minutes, stirring occasionally.

3 Purée the beans in a food processor. Taste and adjust the seasoning. Scrape the mixture back into the sauté pan and keep warm.

divados

Seek out corn tortillas from a Mexican specialty store, mail-order company, or an internet site. Once bought, you can freeze them for up to 4 months. If not available, use flour tortillas, sold in supermarkets. They will produce a more pastry-like texture when fried. Alternatively, flour tortillas can be used for wraps.

Do fry the tortillas up to 2 days ahead and keep in an airtight container. The bean purée can be made up to 1 week ahead. Canned black beans require no soaking and can be used in place of dried.

4 Heat the corn oil in a saucepan or deep-fat fryer. Place one tortilla at a time into the oil using a pair of tongs. Bend the tortilla slightly in half, so that it forms a taco shell. Be careful not to fold it too tight or it will be difficult to get the filling in. Fry for 1 minute until crispy, then drain on paper towels. Repeat until all the tortillas are deep-fried.

5 Mix together all the ingredients for the salsa.

6 To serve, spoon the warm beans into the taco shells and let guests help themselves to salsa and crème fraîche to spoon on top.

The tortillas can also be fried flat to make tostados instead of tacos.

 Serve with Tuna Ceviche or Grilled Shrimp with Tamarind Recado (see pages 32 and 82).

divadon'ts

Don't mix the salsa together until just before serving.

asian potato cakes with tomato sambal

● Makes: 12 cakes   ● Preparation: 50 minutes   ● Cooking: 30 minutes

We're crazy about potato cakes! Deborah Madison of Greens restaurant in San Francisco inspired us years ago into making all kinds of them. This is adapted from one of her ideas.

potato cakes

1 lb 10 oz potatoes, peeled and cut into large chunks

2 medium egg yolks

1¼ cups (4½ oz) cheddar cheese, grated

4 green onions, finely chopped.

1 large handful fresh cilantro, chopped

3 green chilies, deseeded and chopped

salt and pepper

⅔ cup (4½ oz) sesame seeds

2 cups (4½ oz) fresh breadcrumbs

sunflower oil for frying

lime wedges and cilantro sprigs to garnish

tomato sambal

1 quantity Tomato Sambal recipe (see page 22)

1 Cook the potatoes in lightly salted boiling water for about 10 minutes until soft and tender. Drain and leave to dry for 5 minutes.

2 Mash the potatoes with the egg yolks, cheese, green onions, chilantro, chilies, and seasoning to taste. Mix well together.

3 Shape the mixture into 12 medium cakes using lightly floured hands. Mix the sesame seeds and breadcrumbs together. Roll the cakes firmly in the breadcrumb mixture, to coat all over. Chill until needed.

4 Heat 1-inch of oil in a large, non-stick frying pan. Fry the cakes in batches for about 5 minutes, until browned all over. Keep warm in a medium oven.

5 Garnish the potato cakes with lime wedges and sprigs of cilantro. Serve with the tomato sambal.

diva**dos**

This recipe is so versatile – we often make a Mediterranean version, replacing the Cheddar with grated smoked mozzarella, chopped fresh basil in place of the cilantro and 2 oz chopped olives in place of the chilies. Omit the sesame seeds and double the quantity of breadcrumbs. These are excellent served with Chunky Salsa Verde (see page 87).

The potato cakes can be made a day ahead. Fry them one hour before serving and keep warm in a moderate oven.

Ensure that the potatoes are drained really well, otherwise the mixture will be too wet.

You can make these cakes smaller to serve as canapés (makes 24) or top the larger ones with crème fraîche, smoked trout pieces, and little lime wedges to squeeze over.

diva**don'ts**

Do not use a food processor to mash the potatoes, as they will turn to a purée. Mash by hand or using an electric whisk.

couscous with roasted sweet potato and harissa dressing

- Serves: 8   • Preparation: 30 minutes soaking for the couscous and 15 minutes
- cooking: 40 minutes

Harissa is a treasure ingredient brought to us from North Africa. It's a piquant chili paste that's used in everything from salads to grilled fish and meats. We've used it to spice up couscous with roasted vegetables and a lemony vinaigrette. Cool, minty yogurt is drizzled over for a delicious salad or vegetarian main dish.

couscous

10½ oz couscous

1 cup (8 fl oz) vegetable stock

1 lb 9 oz sweet potatoes, peeled and cut into chunks

4 red onions, cut into large chunks

3 red peppers, deseeded and cut into large pieces

½ cup (4 fl oz) extra-virgin olive oil

2 tablespoons balsamic vinegar

1 x 14-oz can chickpeas, drained

salt and pepper

dressing

½ cup (4 fl oz) extra-virgin olive oil

½ cup (4 fl oz) lemon juice

grated zest of 1 lemon

2 teaspoons harissa paste

1 garlic clove, crushed

4 green onions, finely chopped

1 handful of chopped mint, cilantro, and flat-leaf (Italian) parsley

the yogurt sauce

1⅔ cups (14 fl oz) plain greek yogurt

⅓ cup plus 1 tablespoon (3 fl oz) extra-virgin olive oil

¼ cup (2 fl oz) lemon juice

½ teaspoon ground cumin

1 handful of chopped mint, cilantro, and flat-leaf (Italian) parsley

1 Pour the boiling stock over the couscous in a bowl and leave to stand for 30 minutes. Preheat the oven to 400°F.

2 Arrange the sweet potatoes, onions, and peppers in a roasting pan and drizzle with olive oil and vinegar. Roast for 40 minutes. Check after about 30 minutes, as you may need to remove the onions and peppers before the sweet potatoes, if they are already cooked. Leave to cool.

3 Mix all the dressing ingredients in a jar and set aside.

4 Mix together all the ingredients for the yogurt sauce. Chill until needed.

5 Break the couscous up with your fingers so that there are no lumps. Toss with the chickpeas and half of the dressing. Spread onto a large serving platter.

6 Mix the roasted vegetables with the remaining dressing and pile on top of the couscous. Serve the yogurt sauce separately.

divados

You'll find harissa in the specialty or spice sections of some supermarkets. Remember to refrigerate it once opened.

You can make the dressing and yogurt sauce the day before, omitting the herbs until shortly before serving. If making double the quantity of couscous, you'll need twice as much dressing.

Serve with Spicy Shrimp with Tomato Jam or Salad Mezze Plate (see pages 27 and 122). Or you can omit making the yogurt sauce and serve the couscous with our Lamb Fillet with Roasted Garlic, Coriander and Yogurt Sauce (see page 56).

divadon'ts

Don't roast the vegetables more than 4 hours ahead, or they will lose their attractive appearance.

grilled red peppers stuffed with herbed ricotta and black-olive vinaigrette

● Serves: 8   ● Preparation: 2 hours chiling and 50 minutes   ● Cooking: 15 minutes

Stunning peppers packed with a creamy soft cheese, flavored with sweet basil and sharp lemon, then topped off with a vinaigrette dressing, studded with black olives. Sensational!

8 red peppers

filling

8 oz ricotta cheese

8 oz cream cheese

1 tablespoon extra-virgin olive oil

grated zest of 1 lemon

3 large handfuls of fresh basil, chopped

salt and pepper

the vinaigrette

⅓ cup plus 1 tablespoon (3 fl oz) extra-virgin olive oil

2 tablespoons balsamic vinegar

juice of ½ lemon

2 oz pitted black olives, finely chopped

2 garlic cloves, finely chopped

1 teaspoon honey

2 tablespoons chopped basil

a selection of mixed baby leaves to serve

basil leaves to garnish

1 Preheat a hot broiler. Place the whole peppers under the heat and grill them all over, using tongs to turn, until the skins are nicely charred. Remove and place in a plastic bag to cool.

2 Carefully peel away and discard the skins from the peppers, trying not to tear the flesh. Chill until needed.

3 Mix together the filling ingredients, either by hand or in a food processor. Add salt and pepper to taste, then cover and chill for at least 1 hour.

4 Place the vinaigrette ingredients in a screw-top jar and shake well.

5 To fill the peppers, carefully cut them open lengthwise, down one side only, and remove the seeds and membranes. Lay the peppers flat and pat dry inside with paper towels. Spoon the ricotta mixture into the center, dividing it evenly, then neatly roll up. Chill until ready to serve.

6 To serve, scatter the leaves onto a large serving plate (or individual ones), place the peppers on top and drizzle with the vinaigrette. Garnish with basil leaves.

diva**dos**

Any color pepper will work. We love red and don't recommend green, but a mixture of colors would be festive. If desired, add some freshly grated Parmesan cheese to the ricotta filling.

 The peppers can be grilled and skinned and the filling made a day ahead, then covered and kept in the fridge. The peppers can be stuffed 4 hours before serving and chilled. Drizzle with the vinaigrette at the last minute.

diva**don'ts**

We don't advise roasting the peppers. Grilling keeps the flesh of the peppers firm.

babaganoush salad with goat cheese and crispy pita bread

● Serves: 8   ● Preparation: 25 minutes   ● Cooking: about 1 hour

A classic salad from the Middle East is combined with goat cheese to create a powerhouse of flavors. Eat it with our Cumin Flatbread or Diva Breadsticks for a delicious meal.

babaganoush

3 eggplants

2 garlic cloves

juice of 1 lemon

about ⅓ cup (3 oz) tahini (sesame) paste

2 tablespoons extra-virgin olive oil

1 small handful fresh mint

salt and pepper

the crispy pita bread

8 white pita breads

5 tablespoon extra-virgin olive oil

the salad

3 red peppers, halved

2 heads romaine lettuce

4 plum tomatoes, quartered or 8 cherry tomatoes, halved

2 red onions, thinly sliced

1¼ lb goat cheese log, crumbled or sliced

½ cup (4 fl oz) extra-virgin olive oil, plus a little extra if grilling cheese

juice of 1 lemon

1 teaspoon honey

1 Preheat the oven to 375°F. Place the whole eggplants on a baking sheet, prick several times and roast in the preheated oven for 30–40 minutes until blackened and soft. Remove and allow to cool.

2 Slice the core end off the eggplants and peel away and discard the skins. Place the eggplant flesh in a food processor with the remaining babaganoush ingredients. Blend to a purée. Adjust seasoning to taste.

3 Cut the pita breads into large chunks and toss with the olive oil, salt and pepper in a large bowl. Spread on a baking sheet and bake at the same temperature for 10 minutes or until crisp.

4 Preheat a hot broiler. Place the peppers, skin side uppermost, under the heat and grill until the skins have blackened. Remove and place in a

plastic bag to cool. When cool, peel off the skins and discard, and cut the peppers into thick strips.

5 To assemble the salad, arrange the lettuce leaves on a large platter. Top with the tomatoes, onions, and peppers, and then pile up the babaganoush in the center. You can then scatter the crumbled goat cheese over the top or cut the cheese into thick slices and warm it under a grill.

6 To grill the cheese, place the slices on a baking sheet, drizzle with a little olive oil, and sprinkle with pepper. Grill for a few minutes until the cheese starts to brown and bubble. Arrange on top of the salad.

7 Whisk together the olive oil, lemon juice, honey, and seasoning, and spoon the vinaigrette over the leaves. Serve the crispy pita bread in a basket.

diva**dos**

Feta could be used instead of goat cheese.

The crispy pita can be made one day ahead and stored in an airtight container.

The eggplants can be roasted over a barbecue, turning regularly. This adds a lovely smoky flavor.

Don't bother with cutlery – this is so divine you can just scoop it up with the pita and crispy lettuce.

gratin of balsamic wild mushrooms

- Serves: 8 - Preparation: 15 minutes - Cooking: 15 minutes

Wild mushrooms in a rich and creamy balsamic sauce, covered with a crunchy topping of breadcrumbs, Parmesan cheese, and fresh herbs. Bliss!

mushroom mixture

¼ cup (4 fl oz) extra-virgin olive oil

½ lb pied de mouton (hedgehog) mushrooms, chopped

¾ lb Portobello mushrooms, (or any dark, mild flavored mushroom) halved

4½ oz fresh shiitake mushrooms, stemmed and quartered

4 shallots, finely chopped

4 garlic cloves, finely chopped

salt and pepper

¼ cup (2 fl oz) balsamic vinegar

½ cup (4 fl oz) dry white wine

1 cup (8 fl oz) crème fraîche

topping

¾ cup (1½ oz) fresh white breadcrumbs

1½ oz Parmesan cheese cheese, finely grated

1 oz Provolone or Gruyère cheese, finely grated

1 tablespoon chopped thyme

1 tablespoon chopped basil

3 tablespoons chopped flat-leaf (Italian) parsley

1 To prepare the topping, mix together all the ingredients in a bowl, season with salt and pepper and set aside.

2 For the mushroom mixture, heat the olive oil in a large saucepan on a medium-high heat. Add the pied de mouton and chestnut mushrooms, and gently sauté for 3 minutes. Add the shiitake mushrooms, shallots, garlic, salt, and pepper, and sauté for a further 3 minutes. Add the balsamic vinegar and cook for a few minutes until reduced by half.

3 Remove the mushrooms with a slotted spoon and place in a bowl. Reduce the heat and add the wine and crème fraîche to the juices in the pan. Heat gently, without allowing the sauce to boil, for about 5 minutes until thickened and reduced. Adjust seasoning to taste and return the mushrooms to the sauce.

4 Preheat a hot broiler. Pour the mushrooms into an ovenproof dish or individual ramekins and sprinkle the breadcrumb mixture over the top. Grill for 5 minutes or till crispy and golden. Serve hot.

diva**dos**

Pied de Mouton are particularly good mushrooms to use because with their meaty texture they don't go soft quickly. However, any wild mushrooms, such as girolles, chanterelles or field mushrooms, can be substituted. If you're feeling dangerous, use a bit of black truffle shaved over the top. Make this dish in autumn or winter, when wild mushrooms are in season.

The mushroom mixture and topping can both be prepared a day ahead, then chilled. Bring to room temperature before baking.

Grill the mushrooms just before serving to guests. Serve with a salad of radicchio (Italian chicory), endive (escarole), and arugula tossed with Classic Vinaigrette (see page 118).

goat cheese baked in a spicy tomato sauce with garlic crostini

● Serves: 8 ● Preparation: 15-20 minutes ● Cooking: about 1 hour

Creamy goat cheese is baked with an intensely flavored, roasted tomato sauce. Garlicky crostini are used to scoop up delicious mouthfuls.

tomato sauce

2¼ lb ripe plum tomatoes, halved

4 tablespoons extra-virgin olive oil

2 tablespoons balsamic vinegar

3 tablespoons honey

4 garlic cloves, finely chopped

2 teaspoons dried crushed chilies

5-6 thyme sprigs

3 tablespoons tomato paste

salt and pepper

crostini

1 large stick of French bread, cut into 16 thick slices

¼ cup (2 fl oz) extra-virgin olive oil

1 whole garlic clove, peeled

9 oz fresh goat cheese log, with rind

1 Preheat the oven to 400°F. Place the tomato halves on a shallow baking sheet. Drizzle with the olive oil, balsamic vinegar, and honey, then sprinkle with the garlic, chilies, half the thyme, and seasoning. Bake for 30 minutes.

2 Place the roasted tomatoes in a food processor and blend. Add the tomato paste, then taste and add more honey if needed, and salt and pepper to taste.

3 Preheat a hot broiler. To make the crostini, brush each slice of bread with olive oil, then grill until golden and crispy. Rub the clove of garlic over each slice.

4 Place the tomato sauce in a medium-sized, ovenproof baking dish or 8 individual ramekins. Slice the goat cheese into rounds and place on top of the sauce. Drizzle with a little olive oil, strip the leaves from the remaining thyme sprigs and sprinkle over the top with some black pepper.

5 Bake at 400°F for 10-15 minutes until the cheese turns brown on top and the sauce is warm. To serve, place the dish in the center of a large plate and arrange the garlic crostini around the edge.

divados

The tomato sauce can be made well ahead and frozen, or make several days before and chill. Make the crostini up to 2 days before and store in an airtight container.

Bake the dish with the goat cheese topping just before serving.

 Serve as a starter before Spiedini of Scallops with Chunky Salsa Verde (see page 87) or simply with Diva Breadsticks (see page 158) and a spinach, radicchio (Italian chicory), and crouton salad with a gutsy vinaigrette.

divadon'ts

Don't use tomatoes that aren't ripened enough. Buy them at least 4 days before using.

diva**salads**

grilled mediterranean chicken salad with roasted garlic and basil dressing

● Serves: 8   ● Preparation: 30 minutes   ● Cooking: 1 hour

Invented for sunny days, this perfectly balanced salad, with its vibrantly green, gutsy dressing, represents the Mediterranean at its best.

8 boneless, skinless chicken breasts

juice of 1 lemon

½ lb (8 oz) string beans, trimmed

3 red peppers, halved and deseeded

1 red onion, thinly sliced

about ⅓ cup (3 oz) sun-dried tomatoes, sliced

1 x 14 oz can artichoke hearts, drained and quartered

1 oz pitted black olives, halved

¼ lb (4 oz) baby salad leaves to serve

basil leaves to garnish

roasted garlic and basil dressing

3 garlic bulbs

1 cup (8 fl oz) extra-virgin olive oil

1½ teaspoons Dijon mustard

4 large handfuls fresh basil

4 tablespoons red-wine vinegar

1 teaspoon clear honey

salt and pepper

1 Preheat the oven to 375°F. For the dressing, place the garlic bulbs on a baking sheet, drizzle with a little of the olive oil, then wrap tightly in foil and roast in the preheated oven for 45 minutes, until soft. Remove foil and cool a liitle.

2 Cut the garlic bulbs in half and squeeze out the pulp. Place the pulp in a food processor with all the dressing ingredients except the olive oil. With the motor running, slowly drizzle in the oil to make a thick, green dressing. Season to taste.

3 Heat a heavy ridged griddle pan or broiler and sear the chicken breasts on both sides for 5 minutes, until thoroughly cooked. Remove from the heat, pour on the lemon juice, and set aside.

4 Blanch the beans in salted boiling water for 3 minutes. Drain and refresh under cold water.

5 Preheat a hot broiler. Lay the peppers, skin side up, under the heat and grill for about 10 minutes until charred and blistered. Remove and place in a plastic bag to cool. Skin the peppers and slice each half into quarters.

6 Mix all the vegetables together, except the salad leaves, and toss with half the dressing. Scatter the salad leaves on a large platter and pile the vegetables on top. Slice the chicken on a slant and arrange on the salad, then spoon over the remaining dressing and garnish with basil leaves.

diva**dos**

Fresh artichokes or fresh tomatoes can be used, if preferred. You could also add toasted pine nuts.

If feeding a crowd, grill the chicken for 1 minute on each side, then roast for 10 minutes in a hot oven, sprinkled with lemon juice, olive oil, and seasoning.

vietnamese chopped chicken salad

● Serves: 8   ● Preparation: 15 minutes   ● Cooking: 5 minutes

This refreshing salad is a modern take on the classic Vietnamese pork "larb" salad. We think that chicken breast is lighter, juicier, and more attractive. It has all the classic flavors of sweet, salty, and sour that characterize Southeast Asian food.

6 boneless, skinless chicken breasts, roughly chopped

3 tablespoons peanut oil

1 large red onion, chopped

3 tablespoons grated fresh root ginger

3 small red chilies, deseeded and chopped

1 large handful fresh cilantro, chopped

2 iceberg lettuces, separated into leaves

fresh cilantro leaves to garnish

dressing

¼ cup (2 fl oz) fresh lime juice

½ cup (4 fl oz) fresh lemon juice

4 tablespoons Thai fish sauce (nam pla)

2 tablespoons sugar

salt to taste

1 Place the chicken breasts in a food processor and pulse until finely chopped. Heat the oil in a wok or large frying pan until almost smoking. Cook the chicken for about 5 minutes until it turns white, breaking it up thoroughly with a large fork. Make sure you drain off any excess liquid that comes out of the chicken. Transfer to a bowl and then add the onion, ginger, chilies, and chopped cilantro. Toss well.

2 In a small bowl, combine the lime and lemon juices, fish sauce, sugar, and 2 tablespoons of water. Toss the chicken with this dressing and season to taste.

3 Make a pile of the lettuce leaves, placing a couple on top of each other to create individual "bowls". Just before serving, spoon the chicken salad into the lettuce "bowls" and sprinkle a few cilantro leaves on top.

diva**dos**

Do chop fresh chicken breasts rather than buying pre-chopped chicken.

Serve as a canapé in cucumber cups, on baby lettuce leaves or in Wonton Cups (see page 31), or as part of an Oriental menu with Asian Potato Cakes, Roast Fillet of Beef and Shrimp Dumplings in Fragrant Thai Broth (see pages 104, 66 and 88).

diva**don'ts**

Don't make the chicken mixture more than 2 hours ahead, or the onion will dominate the flavor.

dressings and vinaigrettes

When it comes to dressings and vinaigrettes, a little goes a long way!
Most of these ingredients are used sparingly and will last well in your
cupboard or pantry. Simply following recipes is difficult, because everyone's
palate is different, so pour your ingredients into a lidded jar, shake, and taste!

OILS

Extra-Virgin Olive Oil: For vinaigrettes and drizzling. When mixing vinaigrettes, start with ⅓ vinegar and ⅔ oil, then adapt to taste.

Olive Oil: For searing, marinades, and lighter dressings. If you are heating foods, use olive oil.

Walnut Oil: Partner with fruit, nuts, and cheese. Great winter oil.

Hazelnut Oil: Similar to walnut oil, but more powerful.

Sunflower Oil: For mayonnaise or mixed with extra-virgin olive oil to give a lighter touch.

MUSTARDS

Dijon: A great emulsifier, and helps create a creamy, nutty flavor. Excellent for use in Mediterranean dressings. Make sure you use it sparingly, however, as the flavor should not be dominant.

Whole Grain: Sharp flavor and texture. Good for potatoes, mayonnaises, and meat salads.

VINEGARS

Cabernet Sauvignon: Gives dressings an intense red-wine flavor, ideal for sharp vinaigrettes. A key ingredient in Greek salads.

Sherry: Strong, smoky, and nutty aroma. Excellent when paired with walnut oil. Try on bitter lettuces, for example, radicchio (Italian chicory), with some pancetta.

Red Wine: Is this the world's most versatile vinegar? Try adding ½ teaspoon of sugar to create a simple vinaigrette.

Balsamic: Sweet; complements the majority of Mediterranean foods. Excellent mixed with light soy sauce and ginger.

Rice Wine: For oriental dressings.

Cider: Workhorse for hearty fare; wonderful in potato salads.

Champagne: Elegant and light; good with peppery greens.

CITRUS FRUITS

Lemon: The rind and juice are both key ingredients for *agrodolce* flavor – that wonderful sweet-and-sour taste.

Lime: Absolutely essential component of Asian vinaigrettes.

Orange: To add sweetness, mix it with lemon or lime.

FLAVORS

Honey: A little honey goes a long way. It partners well with red-wine vinegar, sherry vinegar, citrus-fruit juice, and Asian salad vinaigrettes.

Pomegranate Molasses: The magic ingredient for Middle Eastern salads, particularly those containing green beans, eggplant, lamb, duck,

couscous and bulgar wheat. Mix, in place of vinegar, with oil, lemon juice, and sugar to make a delicious dressing.

Soy Sauce: Asian essential. Use with balsamic vinegar and sunflower oil to make an oriental vinaigrette.

Fish Sauce: Southeast Asia's powerhouse ingredient; pair with sugar and lime.

DAIRY

Blue Cheese: A sublime partner for bitter chicory, escarole, or potatoes. To make a classic blue-cheese dressing, crumble into crème fraîche with lemon, salt, and pepper. Great on crunchy iceberg lettuce or a grilled steak.

Parmesan Cheese: Nutty, salty, and creamy. Only buy Parmesan stamped *Parmigiano reggiano*; this means it is authentic and has been aged two years.

Yogurt: A light and healthy option for Middle Eastern salads – although we prefer Greek yogurt, which is the creamiest variety.

Crème Fraîche: Creamy partner for potatoes, ham, or bacon in salads. Don't substitute the low-fat variety, since it lacks depth of flavor.

FRESH HERBS

Basil: Delicious in Mediterranean or Asian dressings.

Chives: Complement red-wine or sherry-vinegar dressings; great on salads with meat or potatoes.

Flat-leaf (Italian) Parsley: Superior to the curly variety, this versatile herb is brilliant in all Mediterranean dressings.

Cilantro: Used in Asian, Mexican, and Mediterranean dressings, cilantro is great in chili-lime vinaigrettes.

Tarragon: The French variety has a better flavor than the Russian. Terrific accompaniment to potato salads.

Oregano: Use on tomatoes drizzled with olive oil and red-wine vinegar.

SPICES

Cumin: Smoky-flavored spice for Mexican or Middle Eastern dressings.

Coriander Seeds: Best crushed when used in dressings. Go well with yogurt dressings. A fresh supply is vital, as they lose flavor with time.

Fennel Seeds: Best crushed or ground when used in dressings. Complements Mediterranean salads best.

Chili: A little kick is a great addition, but use sparingly. Different varieties have different strengths. Above all, don't mask the flavor of the food.

Sea Salt: We beg you not to use bleached table salt! Sea salt enhances and softens vegetables when used in cooking. Add salt at the beginning of cooking, not the end, or the dish will taste like you added salt.

Black Pepper: Freshly ground gives the best flavor and texture.

PIQUANT FLAVORS

Olives: Only buy pitted, high-quality olives soaked in olive oil.

Capers: Try to buy salt-packed. Rinse and soak in warm water for 5 minutes in order to remove salt. When chopped to a rough paste, capers add a magical depth to vinaigrettes.

Anchovies: Buy the variety that comes in olive oil. People who swear they hate them will swoon over a dish in which they aren't visible. Rinse with cool water and chop to a fine paste.

Vine-ripened tomatoes: These are only partially dried, leaving them intense yet still moist. Chop finely for a gorgeous Mediterranean vinaigrette.

master recipes for vinaigrettes and mayonnaise

classic mayonnaise Makes: 1¼ cups (10 fl oz)

2 tablespoons white-wine vinegar

2 egg yolks, at room temperature

1 tablespoon Dijon mustard

1 tablespoon soft brown sugar

½ teaspoon each of salt and pepper

1 cup (8 fl oz) sunflower oil

1 Combine all the ingredients, except for the oil, in a blender or food processor. Then, with the motor running, slowly drizzle in the oil until it is all incorporated.

2 This mayonnaise will keep for 4 days in the fridge.

variations

• Add 1 teaspoon saffron threads soaked in 2 tablespoons hot water.

• Add 3–4 finely chopped garlic cloves for a garlic mayonnaise (aïoli).

• Add any chopped fresh herbs, such as tarragon, rosemary, basil, or cilantro.

classic vinaigrette Makes: just over ½ cup (5 fl oz)

1 shallot, finely chopped

1 teaspoon Dijon mustard

4 tablespoons red-wine vinegar (sherry, Cabernet Sauvignon, or balsamic can also be used)

⅓ cup plus 1 tablespoon (3 fl oz) extra-virgin olive oil

1 garlic clove, finely chopped

salt and pepper

1 Place all the ingredients in a screw-top jar and shake well together. Season to taste with salt and pepper.

2 This will keep for 1 week in the fridge. Bring to room temperature and shake well before using.

variations

• Add chopped capers,

• or finely chopped hard-boiled egg,

• or finely chopped anchovies,

• or finely chopped fresh herbs, such as basil or oregano.

classic oriental dressing makes: just over ½ cup (5 fl oz)

2 tablespoons rice-wine vinegar

2 tablespoons light soy sauce

2 tablespoons fresh lime juice

1 tablespoon peanut oil

1 tablespoon sugar

1 garlic clove, finely chopped

1 green onion, finely chopped

a small bunch of fresh cilantro, chopped

1 Place all ingredients in a screw-top jar and shake well together.

2 This will keep for 1 week in the fridge. Shake well before using.

variations

• Add grated fresh root ginger,

• or chopped fresh herbs, such as Thai basil or mint leaves,

• or mirin in place of the rice-wine vinegar,

• or about 1 tablespoon Thai fish sauce,

• or grated lime zest.

soba noodle salad with roasted eggplant and soy-balsamic dressing

• Serves: 8   • Preparation: 25 minutes   • Cooking: 35 minutes

So many noodle salads look tasty, but are dry and bland. This was inspired by a recipe in Deborah Madison's *Greens* cookbook. It's one of the few oriental noodle salads that has depth and taste.

1 lb 10 oz eggplant (small if possible)

1 lb 2 oz Japanese soba noodles

10 asparagus spears, cut diagonally into 1-inch pieces

4 tablespoons sesame seeds, toasted

fresh cilantro leaves to garnish

soy-balsamic dressing

½ cup (4 fl oz) sesame oil

½ cup (4 fl oz) light soy sauce

6 tablespoons balsamic vinegar

6 tablespoon sugar

2 tablespoons chili pepper oil

2 garlic cloves, finely chopped

3 tablespoons grated fresh root ginger

15 green onions, finely sliced

1 small handful of fresh cilantro, finely chopped

1 Preheat the oven to 400°F. Prick the eggplants several times with a sharp knife, then bake for 25 minutes (or longer), until soft. Remove, slice in half lengthwise, and leave to cool. Peel away and discard the skins. Roughly chop the flesh and leave to drain in a colander.

2 Mix together all the dressing ingredients. Dress the chopped eggplant with half the dressing and reserve the rest.

3 Cook the noodles in salted boiling water for about 5 minutes until

al dente. Drain and rinse under cold water. Place in a large bowl, pour on the remaining dressing, and mix evenly, using your fingers.

4 Blanch the asparagus in a large pan of salted boiling water. Drain and refresh in cold water, drain again and pat dry with paper towels. Toss the asparagus with the noodles, eggplant, and sesame seeds. Garnish with cilantro leaves.

diva**dos**

 Chinese egg noodles can be used in place of soba noodles. Do seek out small eggplants – they are less bitter than the larger ones. If not available, use long, firm, and shiny-skinned eggplants.

Make the dressing the day before and the salad on the morning of the party.

Serve with other refreshing dishes, such as Seared Thai Chicken with Tomato-Chili Jam (see page 80).

thai green papaya salad with seared chili shrimp

● Serves: 8 ● Preparation: 1 hour marinating and 30 minutes ● cooking: 2 minutes

This classic Thai salad normally includes tiny dried shrimp, but as these are not easily found or admired by all, we have jazzed it up with gloriously marinated and seared jumbo shrimp.

40 raw jumbo shrimps, peeled

marinade

1 tablespoon chili sauce

1 teaspoon clear honey

1 teaspoon grated fresh root ginger

juice and grated zest of 1 lime

1 tablespoon extra-virgin olive oil,
for searing

salad

1 large green papaya, peeled,
deseeded and grated into long strips

10 snow peas, cut into julienne strips

3 tomatoes, deseeded and diced

2 garlic cloves, finely chopped

½ teaspoon crushed red chilies

1 oz roasted peanuts, chopped

1 tablespoon sugar

2 tablespoons Thai fish sauce
(nam pla)

2 tablespoons fresh lime juice

fresh cilantro sprigs to garnish

1 Mix together the chili sauce, honey, ginger, lime juice, and zest, pour over the shrimp, and leave to marinate for 1 hour.

2 Place the strips of papaya in a large bowl with the snow-peas, tomatoes, garlic, and crushed chilies. Set aside.

3 Preheat a heavy griddle or frying pan, add the olive oil, and sear the shrimp for about 2 minutes, until pink.

4 Add the peanuts, sugar, fish sauce, and lime juice to the papaya mixture, taste and add a little more of any of the flavoring ingredients, if desired.

5 Pile the salad on to a large serving plate, place the seared shrimp around the edge, and garnish with cilantro sprigs.

diva**dos**

This salad can be made with deseeded cucumber cut into thin strips in place of the papaya, although it's not quite the same (cucumber is very watery). The salad also works well with scallops instead of shrimp.

The salad can be prepared a day ahead, but do not add the peanuts or dressing until 30 minutes before you are ready to serve.

The shrimp can be served hot or cold, or even mixed into the salad, once cold. Julienned red chili or green onion also makes an attractive garnish. Serve with Seared Thai Chicken or Grilled Indonesian Coconut Chicken (see pages 80 and 78).

salad mezze plate

● Serves: 8　● Preparation: 1¼ hours　● Cooking: 35 minutes

Mezze, like antipasti, is a flavorful selection of "little dishes". It's a great way to start a party and have everyone digging in and enjoying a colorful feast.

eggplant purée

2 large eggplants

3 tablespoons extra-virgin olive oil

½ cup (4 oz) Greek yogurt

grated zest and juice of ½ lemon

1 small handful of mint, stalks removed

2 garlic cloves

½ teaspoon ground allspice

salt and pepper

chickpea salad

1 x 14 oz can chickpeas, drained

2 red chilies, deseeded and finely chopped

1 red onion, finely chopped

1 small handful fresh cilantro, finely chopped

1 small handful mint, finely chopped

juice of ½ lemon

1 garlic clove, finely chopped

1 tablespoon pomegranate molasses

4 tablespoons extra-virgin olive oil

1 teaspoon cumin seeds, toasted

salt and pepper

3 oz feta cheese, to garnish

fresh cilantro leaves, to garnish

eggplant purée

1 Preheat the oven to 375°F. Prick the eggplants several times with a fork, place in a roasting pan and roast for 35 minutes until blistered and softened. Remove and allow to cool. Cut off the stems, and peel away and discard the skins.

2 Place the eggplant pulp in a food processor with all the remaining ingredients. Purée until smooth. Cover and keep cool until needed.

chickpea salad

1 Place the chickpeas in a food processor and pulse until just crushed. Remove and place in a large bowl with the rest of the ingredients. Stir well and season to taste.

2 Garnish with the crumbled feta and sprinkle with the cilantro leaves.

grilled pepper salad

3 red and 3 orange peppers, quartered and deseeded

1 tablespoon harissa paste or chili sauce

5 tablespoonss extra-virgin olive oil

¼ cup (1½ oz) pitted black olives, chopped

½ cup (2 oz) toasted pine nuts, chopped

1 small handful of basil, thinly sliced

salt and pepper

1 Preheat a hot broiler. Grill the peppers until the skins have blackened, then place in a plastic bag to cool.

2 Mix the harissa and olive oil together. Skin the peppers and cut the flesh into thick slices. Place in a bowl and add the harissa oil, olives, pine nuts, basil, and seasoning.

diva**dos**

 Serve with either our Cumin Flatbread or Pita Breadsticks (see pages 163 and 11) or with other great Mediterranean dishes like Lamb Fillet with Roasted Garlic, Coriander and Yogurt or Pomegranate-marinated Lamb Cutlets with Coriander Tabbouleh (see pages 56 and 59).

tuscan panzanella salad

● Serves: 8   ● Preparation: 45 minutes   ● Cooking: 7 minutes

Panzenella is not often seen in restaurants outside of Tuscany. Lush cherry tomatoes, crunchy cucumber, capers, and chewy bread create a myriad punchy flavors and textures. It's a wonderful salad for summer when the vegetables are at their peak.

1 large Italian ciabatta or sourdough loaf, sliced and cut into bite-sized chunks

10½ oz cherry tomatoes, halved

3 celery stalks, sliced

3 red peppers, roasted, peeled and sliced into strips

10 Italian black olives, pitted and halved

3 tablespoons capers, well-rinsed

1 large red onion, finely chopped

2 mini cucumbers (or 1 large cucumber, deseeded), peeled and diced large

2 handfuls of basil, sliced

1 garlic clove, finely chopped

1 anchovy, rinsed and chopped

the dressing

½ cup (4 fl oz) extra-virgin olive oil

½ cup (4 fl oz) red-wine vinegar (Cabernet Sauvignon) or balsamic vinegar

salt and pepper

8 halved fresh anchovies to garnish (optional)

1 Preheat the oven to 400°F. Place the bread on a baking sheet, drizzle with a little olive oil, and sprinkle with seasoning. Bake for 7 minutes, or until crispy. Remove and allow to cool.

2 Combine all the ingredients, except the dressing, in a large salad bowl.

3 When ready to serve, pour on the oil and vinegar, sprinkle with salt and pepper, and garnish, if desired, with the fresh anchovies.

diva**dos**

Do use ripe cucumbers and tomatoes, since flavor is important in this salad. Plum or vine-ripened tomatoes, cut into chunks, can replace the cherry tomatoes. Fresh anchovies, from a deli, are pure white in color and look and taste nothing like the canned variety.

The croutons can be made a day ahead and stored in an airtight container. The vegetables should not be sliced more than 4 hours ahead, then not combined until ready to serve.

Serve with other great Mediterranean dishes during the summer, like Slow-roasted Tuscan Pork, Lamb Fillet with Roasted Garlic, Coriander and Yogurt or Brochettes of Lemon Chicken (see pages 57, 56 and 73).

marinated fig, glazed shallot, and prosciutto salad with parmesan chips

● Serves: 8   ● Preparation: 4 hours marinating and 30 minutes   ● Cooking: 50 minutes

Our passion for cooking with figs and creating new salads was how this stunning recipe was invented. The crunchy Parmesan chips and prosciutto are wonderful with the luscious figs.

8 fresh ripe figs, quartered

2 tablespoons extra-virgin olive oil

1 tablespoon balsamic vinegar

16 small shallots, peeled

1 teaspoon golden sugar

3 oz Parmesan cheese, freshly grated

8 slices of prosciutto

6 oz arugula leaves or watercress, to serve

the vinaigrette

1 teaspoon Dijon mustard

1 garlic clove, finely chopped

1 small red onion, finely chopped

2 tablespoons balsamic vinegar

1 cup (8 fl oz) extra-virgin olive oil

salt and pepper

1 Place the figs on a plate, sprinkle with half the olive oil and vinegar and leave to marinate for about 4 hours.

2 Preheat the oven to 350°F. Place the shallots in a roasting pan, drizzle with the remaining oil and vinegar, sprinkle with sugar and seasoning, then roast for 40 minutes, regularly shaking the pan. Remove and set aside. Increase the temperature to 375°F.

3 To make the Parmesan chips, line 2 baking sheets with non-stick baking parchment paper and sprinkle the Parmesan cheese evenly into 2 x 8-inch circles. Bake for 3 minutes, until bubbling. Remove rom the oven, cool for 1 minute, then slice each circle into 4 triangles.

Separate the triangles slightly on the non-stick baking parchment paper, then return to the oven for another 3 minutes until golden. Remove and cool on a wire rack. Handle with care!

4 Lay the prosciutto directly on to a baking sheet and roast at the same temperature for 5 minutes to crisp. Cool on paper towels.

5 Whisk together the vinaigrette ingredients. Season to taste.

6 To serve, pile the arugula leaves on individual plates and divide the figs and shallots among them. Place the prosciutto on top, spoon on the vinaigrette, and garnish each serving with a Parmesan chip.

diva**dos**

Parma, serrano or Bayonne ham can also be used, or even rashers of bacon. Add your favorite blue cheese to this salad for a delicious variation. Caramelized quartered red onions can replace the glazed shallots.

The Parmesan chips can be made a day ahead. Store in an airtight container. Make the vinaigrette several days ahead and keep in a screw-top jar. Roast the shallots one day ahead – do not chill.

Parmesan chips are so simple, but keep an eye on them since the cooking time may vary slightly for different ovens.

Assemble no more than 20 minutes before serving. This makes an elegant appetizer before Spiedini of Scallops or Butterflied Leg of Lamb (see pages 87 and 64).

thai beef salad

● Serves: 8   ● Preparation: 1 hour marinating and 30 minutes   ● cooking: 20 minutes

This classic Thai dish has been very popular recently for a very good reason: it's so delicious! Healthy and bursting with flavor, we think it's the best combination we've ever tasted.

2¼ lb lean beef fillet or sirloin steak

1 tablespoon Thai fish sauce (nam pla)

2 teaspoons black peppercorns, crushed

20 leaves of romaine lettuce

1 large red onion, thinly sliced

1 lb 2 oz cherry or pomodorino tomatoes, halved

8 mini cucumbers, cut into julienne strips

2 large red chilies, deseeded and cut into julienne strips

fresh cilantro leaves to garnish

vinaigrette

½ cup (4 fl oz) fresh lime juice

2 tablespoons Thai fish sauce (nam pla)

1 teaspoon light soy sauce

1 teaspoon sweet chili sauce

2 teaspoons sugar

1 garlic clove, crushed

1 handful of fresh cilantro, chopped

a handful of mint, chopped

1 lemongrass stalk, thinly sliced

1 Marinate the beef in the fish sauce and peppercorns for at least 1 hour or overnight, covered and chilled.

2 Place all the vinaigrette ingredients in a screw-top jar and shake.

3 Preheat the oven to 400°F. Sear the beef on both sides in a hot frying pan until browned. Transfer to a roasting pan and roast for 15 minutes until just medium-rare. Rest for 10 minutes, then slice thinly.

4 Line a platter with the lettuce leaves. Place the onions, tomatoes, cucumbers, and chilies in a large bowl and toss with half the vinaigrette. Spoon on top of the lettuce leaves.

5 Arrange the beef elegantly around the edge of the platter and spoon the remaining vinaigrette over the meat. Scatter cilantro leaves over the salad to garnish.

diva**dos**

Look for fat, juicy limes by giving them a good squeeze at the shops.

Prepare everything in the morning, then add the dressing just before serving.

The beef can be served hot or cold in this salad.

Serve with Seared Thai Chicken, Thai Green Papaya Salad or Asian Potato Cakes (see pages 80, 120 and 104) for a fabulous Asian feast.

greek chicken salad with caper and anchovy vinaigrette

● Serves: 8 regular servings or 6 greedy ones   ● Preparation: 25 minutes plus 1 hour or overnight marinating   ● Cooking: 10 minutes

Here we've combined creamy feta cheese, and the ripest cucumbers and tomatoes with grilled chicken and an anchovy-spiked dressing.

6 boneless, skinless chicken breasts

marinade

grated zest and juice of 2 lemons

5 tablespoons extra-virgin olive oil

1 teaspoon chopped oregano

salt and pepper

salad

10½ oz cherry or pomodorino tomatoes, halved

1 large red onion, finely chopped

2 mini cucumbers (or 1 large cucumber, deseeded), peeled and sliced

2 tablespoons chopped fresh oregano (or 2 teaspoons dried)

9 oz imported feta cheese, cut into ½–inch cubes

caper and anchovy vinaigrette

2 anchovies in oil, well-rinsed and finely chopped

20 small capers, rinsed and finely chopped

2 garlic cloves, finely chopped

½ cup plus 2 tablespoons (5 fl oz) red-wine vinegar (Cabernet Sauvignon)

¾ cup (6 fl oz) extra-virgin olive oil

1 Combine the ingredients for the marinade and marinate the chicken for at least 1 hour or overnight.

2 Place all the vinaigrette ingredients in a screw-top jar, add seasoning, and shake well.

3 Preheat a heavy ridged grill pan, broiler, or barbecue. Remove the chicken from the marinade and sear

for 5 minutes on each side until cooked through. Remove the chicken, cover and rest for 5 minutes, then carve into thin, diagonal slices.

4 Combine the tomatoes, onion, cucumber, chicken, and oregano in a large bowl. Add the feta.

5 Just before serving, pour on the dressing and toss together.

diva**dos**

 Buy creamy feta cheese imported from Greece or Lebanon. Lebanese and Greek shops are also wonderful sources for mini cucumbers and yogurt. Use ripe cherry tomatoes – they are far less watery than larger ones. Cabernet Sauvignon vinegar has a unique cherry flavor, but if unavailable, use a good-quality red-wine vinegar.

Prepare the vegetables on the morning of the party. The chicken can be served warm or cold. If served cold, it can be cooked the day before, chilled, and covered.

diva**extras**

tamarind-roasted vegetables

• Serves: 8 • Preparation: 20 minutes • Cooking: 45 minutes

Move over potatoes: there's a new side dish in town. Winter root vegetables, red peppers, and baby corn are sweetened by roasting, then tossed in a spicy tamarind glaze. A perfect partner for Asian dishes – or just for eating on its own with rice.

16 fresh baby corn

4 large sweet potatoes, peeled and cut into ½-inch cubes

3 red, yellow or orange peppers, cut into 1-inch pieces

3 red onions, quartered

4 baby beets, halved (or 2 large beets, quartered)

16 whole shallots, peeled

4 tablespoons peanut oil

tamarind glaze

½ cup (4 fl oz) bottled tamarind purée

3 garlic cloves

2 teaspoons freshly grated ginger

2 lemongrass stalks, peeled of outer layers, top ⅓ removed and chopped

2 medium-sized red chilies, deseeded and chopped

10 mint leaves

1 small handful fresh cilantro (separate stems and leaves)

2 tablespoons clear honey

1 teaspoon each of salt and pepper

1 First make the glaze. Place the tamarind, garlic, ginger, chopped lemongrass, chilies, mint, cilantro stems, honey, and salt and pepper in a food processor. Blend to a purée and taste for seasoning. Add extra honey if desired.

2 Preheat the oven to 400°F. Place the vegetables on a large baking sheet (or use 2 smaller sheets), toss with

the peanut oil, and season with salt and pepper. Bake for 30 minutes, then remove from the oven.

3 Pour on the tamarind mixture, mix with the vegetables, then place back in the oven. Roast for a further 15 minutes, until nicely glazed.

4 Garnish with the chopped cilantro leaves.

diva**dos**

If desired, you can replace the sweet potatoes with butternut squash or pumpkin. Make your own tamarind purée by soaking a chunk of tamarind pulp in warm water and sieving the liquid. Be sure to keep it refrigerated.

The vegetables can be chopped the day before and the tamarind glaze made up to 2 days ahead.

Serve these vegetables as a main course meal with Fragrant Coconut Rice (see page 139) or with any Asian dishes like Korean Barbecued Chicken (see page 71), as a perfect complement.

diva**don'ts**

Do not overcrowd the baking sheets with vegetables or they will produce too much steam and won't crisp.

mashed sweet potatoes and ginger

● Serves: 8   ● Preparation: 10 minutes   ● Cooking: 25 minutes

We love sweet potatoes for their vibrant color and sweet, creamy taste.
This is a stunning dish to serve with any Asian or Mediterranean meal.

2½ lb orange sweet potatoes, peeled
and cut into large chunks

¼ cup (2 oz) butter

2-inch piece of fresh root ginger,
grated

2 tablespoons olive oil

salt and pepper

chopped fresh cilantro to garnish

1 Place the sweet potato chunks
in a saucepan of lightly salted,
cold water. Bring to a boil, then
reduce the heat, cover, and simmer
for 20 minutes, until tender. Drain
well in a colander.

2 While the potatoes are draining,
melt the butter in the pan and add the
grated ginger. Soften for 5 minutes,
then return the potatoes to the pan.
Add the olive oil and seasoning.
Mash until soft.

3 Serve hot, scattered with lots
of cilantro.

diva**dos**

 We recommend using the most
common sweet potato with
orange/brown skin and bright
orange flesh. Be careful not to buy
the purple, white-fleshed sweet
potato – it has a poor color and
tastes far too sweet. You can also
use butternut squash instead of
sweet potato.

This recipe can be prepared the
day before, then reheated.

Sweet potatoes are excellent baked
and roasted as well as boiled.

 Serve with poultry dishes like
Braised Duck Legs with Soy,
Ginger and Star Anise or Seared
Duck Breasts with Balsamic
Vinegar, Rosemary and Shallot
Sauce (see pages 68 and 74).

celeriac and roasted garlic purée

● Serves: 8   ● Preparation: 10 minutes   ● Cooking: 1 hour

We always look forward to winter because we get to cook root vegetables again. With their earthy, sweet flavors, they are wonderful in purées or roasted until crisp. Here, we've combined creamy celeriac with nutty roasted garlic to make a classic purée for cold weather.

3 garlic bulbs

3 tablespoons olive oil

2¼ lb celeriac, peeled and cut into large chunks

3 tablespoons crème fraîche

¼ teaspoon ground nutmeg

1 tablespoon chopped thyme

salt and pepper

chopped flat-leaf (Italian) parsley to garnish

1 To prepare the garlic purée, preheat the oven to 375°F. Place the whole garlic bulbs on a large sheet of aluminum foil, and drizzle with the olive oil. Seal the foil thoroughly and roast for 1 hour. Then open the foil and allow the garlic to cool a little. Cut the top third off the bulbs and squeeze out all the pulp from each. Discard the skins.

2 Meanwhile, place the celeriac in a saucepan of cold, lightly salted water. Cover, bring to a boil, and simmer for about 30 minutes, until tender.

3 Drain the celeriac thoroughly, then place in a food processor with the garlic pulp, crème fraiche, nutmeg, thyme, and seasoning. Purée until smooth. Serve hot, sprinkled with chopped parsley.

divados

This recipe also works well with parsnip, yellow turnips, or pumpkin, or try roasted garlic added to mashed potato – it tastes fantastic!

You can make this the day before, then reheat to serve.

This purée is excellent served with Slow-roasted Tuscan Pork or Guinea Fowl Breasts with Tarragon (see pages 57 and 70).

divadon'ts

Do not undercook the celeriac. Unlike potatoes, it takes quite a long time to cook through properly.

moroccan carrots

● Serves: 8   ● Preparation: 15 minutes   ● Cooking: 5 minutes

If you've never had this classic North African salad, you are missing out on one of life's greatest pleasures. Baby carrots are bathed in a zesty vinaigrette with copious amounts of paprika, parsley, and garlic. They make a great addition to mezze or can be eaten, slightly mashed, with pita bread.

1 lb 10 oz whole baby carrots, trimmed and peeled

the vinaigrette

½ cup (4 fl oz) extra-virgin olive oil

⅓ cup plus 1 tablespoon (3 fl oz) red-wine vinegar (Cabernet Sauvignon)

2 tablespoons sweet paprika (preferably *pimentón*)

2 tablespoons ground cumin

3 garlic cloves, finely chopped

1 small handful of fresh flat-leaf (Italian) parsley, finely chopped

1 teaspoon each of salt and pepper

1 To make the vinaigrette, mix together the olive oil, vinegar, paprika, cumin, garlic, parsley, and salt and pepper.

2 Cook the carrots in lightly salted boiling water for 5 minutes, until just tender. Drain immediately.

3 Toss the carrots with the vinaigrette and leave to stand at room temperature for 4 hours before serving, or chill overnight.

diva**dos**

If preferred, large carrots can be used and sliced into 2-inch batons. If using baby carrots, add a glamorous touch by leaving on a little of the green tops.

Make this salad 1–2 days before your party. This will improve the flavor significantly.

This dish would go well with Lamb Fillet with Roasted Garlic, Coriander and Yogurt Sauce, Salad Mezze Plate, Cumin Flatbread or Filo Tart with Charmoula Chicken (see pages 56, 122, 163, and 52).

diva**don'ts**

Take care not to overcook the carrots, otherwise they will take on a slimy texture.

fennel slaw with dill and cider-vinegar dressing

● Serves: 8　● Preparation: 15 minutes

Too many supermarket delis, with their large tubs of dull coleslaws, have given this salad a seriously downmarket reputation. We've created the new-millennium version with wafer thin fennel, dill, and a tangy dressing spiked with cider vinegar.

1 lb 2 oz fennel bulbs, with cores removed

4½ oz red cabbage

1 small red onion, finely chopped

1 large handful fresh dill, chopped

grated zest of 1 lemon

2 tablespoons sugar

1 teaspoon Tabasco sauce

¼ cup (2 fl oz) Classic Mayonnaise (see page 118)

2 tablespoons cider vinegar

salt and pepper

1 Using a sharp serrated knife, slice the fennel and cabbage as paper-thin as possible, then roughly chop the slices.

2 Combine all the ingredients and season to taste. Cover and chill for at least 1 hour before serving.

diva**dos**

Choose small white fennel bulbs that are not bruised.

The slaw is best made the day before, improving the flavor and crunchy texture.

Delicious served with Spicy Crab Cakes (see page 84).

diva**don'ts**

Don't substitute dried dill. Fresh dill is an essential flavor in this salad.

baby green salad with beets, green onion, and sesame

● Serves: 8   ● Preparation: 15 minutes

A perfect salad to complement an oriental or Mediterranean dish, and good with grilled meat, fish, or poultry.

3 raw beets, peeled

1 lb 2 oz selected baby salad leaves

1 bunch of green onions, trimmed

5 baby red radishes, thinly sliced

2 tablespoons toasted sesame seeds, to garnish

dressing

2 tablespoons rice-wine vinegar

2 teaspoons light soy sauce

1 teaspoon sesame oil

½ teaspoon sugar

1 Slice the beets into thin slices, then cut into fine julienne strips. Toss together the salad leaves, beets, green onions, and radishes.

diva**dos**

Baby spinach and arugula leaves are nice for this salad.

Make the dressing the day before. The salad ingredients can be prepared several hours before serving. Keep covered and chilled. If cutting the beets into julienne strips is too time consuming, it can be grated, although this will make the beets weep and very wet. Washed salad leaves need to be drained and then well-dried.

2 Whisk together the rice-wine vinegar, soy sauce, sesame oil, and sugar. Pour over the salad just before serving and toss together. Sprinkle with the sesame seeds.

caramelized new potatoes with tomato and soy

● Serves: 8 ● Preparation: 10 minutes ● Cooking: 45 minutes

This recipe was invented when we were cooking the Roast Fillet of Beef with Cilantro and Peanut Pesto (see page 66). It was for a large number of people and required an imaginative and tasty side dish. These potatoes worked perfectly and looked like little glistening jewels on the plate.

1 tablespoon light soy sauce

1 tablespoon dark soy sauce

1 tablespoon honey

1 tablespoon olive oil

1 teaspoon tomato paste

½ teaspoon English mustard

a pinch of cayenne pepper

1 lb 10 oz new potatoes, cleaned

¼ cup (1 oz) sesame seeds

a small handful chives, chopped

1 Preheat the oven to 375°F. Mix together the soy sauces, honey, olive oil, tomato paste, mustard, and cayenne pepper. Pour this mixture over the potatoes in a large roasting pan and stir to coat.

2 Place in the oven and roast for 45 minutes, shaking the pan every 15 minutes to prevent sticking. Sprinkle with the sesame seeds 5 minutes before the end of cooking.

3 Remove from the oven and serve sprinkled with chives.

diva**dos**

Use small, round potatoes.

You can prepare the soy glaze mixture the day before.

Coat the potatoes with the glaze just before cooking.

The potatoes are best served hot, straight from the oven. Serve with Roast Fillet of Beef or Miso Glazed Cod (see pages 66 and 92).

diva**don'ts**

The potatoes should not be wet, or the glaze will slip off and burn on the bottom of the roasting pan.

saffron-roasted potatoes with rosemary and red onions

● Serves: 8   ● Preparation: 10 minutes   ● Cooking: 45 minutes

Show-stopper potatoes that suit almost any meat or vegetable dish.

2¼ lb large potatoes, peeled

3 red onions, each cut into 6 wedges

saffron dressing

4 tablespoons boiling water

a large pinch of saffron powder
or threads

grated zest and juice of 2 lemons

5 tablespoons olive oil

6 tablespoons (3 oz) butter, diced

1 teaspoon sugar

3 tablespoons chopped rosemary
(or 2 tablespoons dried)

salt and pepper

1 Preheat the oven to 350°F. Pour boiling water over the saffron and leave to infuse for 5 minutes. Cut the potatoes in half lengthwise, then cut each half into three lengthwise.

2 In a bowl, mix the lemon zest and juice, saffron liquid, olive oil, butter, sugar, rosemary, and salt and pepper.

diva**dos**

Turmeric can be used instead of saffron (use ½ teaspoon), and fresh or dried thyme can replace the rosemary. Use whole shallots instead of red onions.

The dressing can be prepared several hours ahead, then poured over the potatoes and onions just before roasting.

Add an extra drizzle of olive oil or water to the potatoes during roasting if they are getting dry but are not quite cooked.

These potatoes are best served straight from the oven. They are excellent with Butterflied Leg of Lamb with Slow-roasted Tomato, Basil and Olive Confit or Slow-roasted Tuscan Pork (see pages 64 and 57).

3 Place the potatoes and onions in a large roasting pan. Pour over the saffron dressing. Roast for 45 minutes, turning the vegetables every 15 minutes, until tender.

fragrant coconut rice

- Serves: 8   • Preparation: 5 minutes   • Cooking: 15 minutes

Fluffy rice, enhanced with aromatic cinnamon and rich coconut milk, is a great extra for any Asian meal.

3½ cups (28 fl oz) coconut milk (about 2 cans)

½ cup (4 fl oz) water

1 teaspoon grated lemon zest

1 cinnamon stick

2 teaspoons salt

1 lb basmati or jasmine rice

1 Combine the coconut milk, water, lemon zest, cinnamon stick, and salt in a saucepan and slowly bring to a boil.

2 Stir in the rice and reduce the heat to low. Cover the pan and cook gently for 15 minutes, until tender.

3 Stir and check that the rice is cooked. If not, add a little more water and cook for a few more minutes.

4 Take the pan off the heat, remove the cinnamon stick, and cover to keep warm until time to serve.

diva**dos**

This recipe can be made a day ahead. Cool, cover, and chill until needed. Reheat, covered, in a microwave or steamer to keep the rice moist.

If cooking the rice in advance, slightly undercook it so that it doesn't become mushy.

Great served with Seared Thai Chicken with Tomato-Chili Jam, Grilled Indonesian Coconut Chicken or Roasted Winter Vegetables (see pages 80, 78 and 101). The rice looks good served in a large bowl lined with a banana leaf and garnished with large slices of red chili.

diva**don'ts**

Don't rinse the basmati or jasmine rice for this recipe.

diva**desserts**

sweet goat cheese, orange, and almond tart

● Serves: 8   ● Preparation: 30 minutes   ● Cooking: 35 minutes

Even people who normally dislike goat cheese will be persuaded by this dish! This sumptuous tart is especially stunning served warm from the oven with fresh fruit.

9 oz sweet pastry (see Basic Pastry recipe on page 148, but add 1 oz sugar to the flour and omit the salt and pepper)

the filling

9 oz mild soft goat cheese

9 oz cream cheese

½ cup (4 oz) sugar

grated zest of ½ orange

½ teaspoon pure vanilla extract

2 medium eggs, separated

2 tablespoons heavy (whipping) cream

¼ cup (1 oz) flaked almonds

1 Preheat the oven to 375°F. Roll out the pastry and line an 8-inch loose-bottomed tart pan or pie plate. Bake for 10 minutes (see page 48), then remove the baking beans and bake for a further 5 minutes.

2 Beat the cheeses with the sugar, orange zest, and vanilla until smooth. Add the egg yolks, 1 at a time, and then stir in the cream.

3 Whisk the egg whites until stiff, then fold into the goat cheese mixture.

4 Pour into the tart shell and scatter the almonds over the surface.

5 Place the tart in the oven and immediately turn the temperature down to 325°F. Bake for 20 minutes. or until just set. (Don't worry if the tart is still a little wobbly – it will set while cooling.)

diva**dos**

Use a mild, soft goat cheese, which won't have the strong "goaty" flavor the harder ones have.

This tart can be made a day ahead, then reheated for 10 minutes in a low oven.

This is excellent in the summer with soft fruits or in the winter with our Glazed Winter Fruits (see page 147). Serve warm or at room temperature.

diva**don'ts**

Do not chill the cooked tart – the flavor will suffer and the pastry will soften.

honey and mascarpone crème brûlée

- Serves: 8 • Preparation: 20 minutes infusing, several hours chiling, and 20 minutes
- cooking: 45 minutes

Mascarpone cheese and honey give a crème brûlée a surprising twist. It's extremely light and very silky – which is why we think this is the best brûlée ever!

2 medium eggs

3 medium egg yolks

⅓ cup plus 1 tablespoon (3 fl oz) good-quality, fragrant clear honey

1¼ cups (10 fl oz) milk

1¼ cups (10 fl oz) heavy (whipping) cream

2 vanilla pods, split

1 tablespoon grated orange zest

3½ oz mascarpone cheese

½ cup (4 oz) sugar

1 Preheat the oven to 250°F. Whisk the eggs, egg yolks, and honey in a bowl until pale and thick.

2 Heat the milk, cream, vanilla pods, and orange zest in a saucepan over a medium heat. Remove from heat and leave to infuse for 20 minutes.

3 Remove the vanilla pods and scrape the seeds into the creamy milk. Pour the milk over the egg mixture. Add the mascarpone and whisk gently.

4 Strain the mixture into a large jug, then leave to stand for several hours in the fridge.

5 Pour the custard into 8 ramekins, then place in a large roasting pan and half-fill the pan with hot water. Bake for 40 minutes, until just set.

6 Remove and allow to cool, then keep in the fridge until ready to serve.

7 About 30 minutes before serving, spoon the sugar over the crèmes in an even layer. Carefully caramelize the tops using a hand-held blow torch. Leave to stand for a few minutes until the topping has set, then serve immediately.

diva**dos**

Choose the most flavorful honey available.

Make the crèmes the day before. You can "brûlée" them at least 1 hour before serving.

If you do not have a blow torch, buy an inexpensive one at a hardware or good kitchen shop! We find overhead grills are too slow – they tend to "brûlée" the top while melting the base!

Serve alone or with Glazed Winter Fruits (see page 147), summer fruits, or roasted rhubarb. Cut rhubarb into diagonal pieces, place in a non-stick roasting pan, sprinkle with 1–2 tablespoons sugar and roast at 350°F for 5 minutes.

new york cheesecake with fresh blueberries

● Serves: 10   ● Preparation: 4 hours chiling and 15 minutes   ● Cooking: 30-40 minutes

Forget about those gelatine-laden cheesecakes – they're nothing but imposters!
This is true cheesecake with a rich, fudgy texture. It's excellent with any fresh
fruit or eaten all by itself.

base

1½ cups (7 oz) graham
cracker crumbs

¼ cup (2 oz) butter, melted

topping

2¼ lb cream cheese

1¼ cups (9 oz) sugar

2 tablespoons pure vanilla extract

grated zest and juice of 1 lemon

5 medium eggs

4 tablespoons all-purpose flour

9 oz fresh blueberries, to decorate

1 Preheat the oven to 350°. Mix
the cookie crumbs with the melted
butter. Press firmly into a greased
8–9-inch springform pan.

2 Beat the cream cheese and sugar
with an electric mixer. Add the vanilla,
lemon zest, and juice. Mix until
smooth, then add the eggs, one at a
time, until fully blended. Add the flour
and blend again.

3 Pour the mixture into the pan.
Bake for 30–40 minutes, until it's
firm when jiggled and the top is
turning a light golden color. Cool, then
chill in the fridge for at least 4 hours.
Keep the cheesecake in the pan.

4 To serve, remove from the pan
and cover with the blueberries.

diva**dos**

 Use a good-quality cream cheese.
Other types of cookies, like
chocolate or ginger, can replace
the graham crackers.

 Make this up to 2 days ahead so
that the texture is firm.

 Don't worry if a split forms on the
top of the cake; this is normal and
can be covered with a dusting of
confectioner's sugar or fruit.

Serve in thin slices since this is
very rich. In the summer, top with
red berries and decorate with mint
leaves, or in the colder months, top
with Glazed Winter Fruits
(see page 147).

cinnamon pavlovas with caramelized apples and blackberries

- Serves: 8   • Preparation: 30 minutes   • Cooking: 1 hour

Cinnamon and apples are a match made in heaven. We guarantee that a bite of these fragrant pavlovas will bring great delight!

meringue

4 medium egg whites

1 cup (8 oz) sugar

1 teaspoon cornstarch

1 teaspoon pure vanilla extract

1 teaspoon white-wine vinegar

4 teaspoons ground cinnamon

topping

3 Granny Smith apples

¼ cup (2 oz) unsalted butter

½ cup (4 oz) soft brown sugar

3 tablespoons brandy

3½ oz fresh blackberries

1 cup plus 2 tablespoons (9 fl oz) heavy (whipping) cream

1 Preheat the oven to 350°F. Line 2 baking sheets with non-stick baking parchment paper.

2 Whisk the eggs whites until stiff. Gradually whisk in the sugar, a couple of tablespoons at a time, then add the cornstarch, vanilla, vinegar, and cinnamon, and whisk until smooth and glossy.

3 Divide the meringue mixture evenly on the baking sheets into 8 x 5-inch individual circles and make a slight dip in the center of each. Place in the oven and immediately turn down the temperature to 250°F. Bake for 1 hour, until crisp.

4 Meanwhile, peel, core, and cut each apple into 8 thick slices. Gently melt the butter in a saucepan, then add the sugar and stir until dissolved. Add the apples and cook over a medium heat until the apples have softened and caramelized.

5 Just before serving, add the brandy and blackberries to the apples. Whip the cream until stiff.

6 To serve, place a spoonful of cream on top of each meringue and spoon on the warm, caramelized fruit. Serve immediately.

diva**dos**

Leave out the cinnamon and you have the classic pavlova recipe.

Be sure to use egg whites at room temperature, or they will not whisk properly. Make the meringues up to a week before and keep in an airtight container.

To make 1 large pavlova, divide the mixture into 2 x 8-inch round circles. Sandwich together with cream and spoon on the fruit.

Summer berries would be an excellent alternative fruit, with melted chocolate drizzled on top. Use mint leaves to decorate and give extra height.

pistachio and berry meringue roulade

● Serves: 8 ● Preparation: 20 minutes ● Cooking: 15 minutes

We've turned the old, reliable meringue into something quite sublime. Berries and cream are rolled with chewy, nutty meringue for this terrific party dessert.

5 medium egg whites

pinch of salt

1⅓ cups (9 oz) sugar

1¼ cups (3½ oz) unsalted, shelled pistachio nuts, coarsely chopped

1¼ cups (10 fl oz) heavy (whipping) cream

7 oz fresh raspberries

sifted confectioner's sugar and summer berries, to decorate

1 Preheat the oven to 325°F. Line a 10 x 14-inch Swiss roll pan with non-stick baking parchment paper.

2 Whisk the egg whites with the salt until stiff. Gradually whisk in the sugar, a couple of tablespoons at a time. Fold in the pistachio nuts, then spread the mixture evenly in the pan. Bake for 15 minutes, until crisp. Remove from the oven and cool.

3 Whip the cream until stiff, then gently fold in the raspberries.

4 Turn the meringue out onto another sheet of non-stick baking parchment paper, and then carefully peel away the lining paper.

5 Spread the berry cream evenly over the meringue, then roll up lengthwise. Dust with confectioner's sugar and decorate with berries. Serve cut into slices.

diva**dos**

Any soft fruit, fruit curd, or berries can be used in the filling. A mixture of Greek yogurt with cream is also delicious. You can buy unsalted, shelled pistachio nuts in the baking section of most supermarkets.

Make the meringue a day ahead. Fill and roll, and keep in the fridge up to 6 hours before serving.

Do not cook the meringue for more than 20 minutes – overcooking will make it hard to roll. Don't worry if the meringue isn't crisping; it will, once removed from the oven.

glazed winter fruits

● Serves: 8 ● Preparation: 10 minutes ● Cooking: 15 minutes

Winter fruit, such as apples and pears, is perfect for glazing with butter, brown sugar, and brandy, especially if you have underripe fruit. Serve with crisp, nutty biscotti and crème fraîche.

4 Granny Smith apples

3 firm pears

4 firm, dark plums

¼ cups (2 oz) unsalted butter

½ cup (4 oz) soft brown sugar or sugar

2 tablespoons brandy or Armagnac

1 Peel the apples and pears, core and cut into thick slices. Halve the plums, remove the stones, and cut into quarters.

2 Melt the butter in a large frying pan, add the sugar and stir a little to dissolve, allowing the sugar to darken a little.

3 Add the apples and pears. Cook, stirring continuously, for 5 minutes, or until the fruit has begun to soften. Add the plums and continue cooking gently for 3–5 minutes, until the fruit has glazed and softened.

4 Just before serving, add the brandy or Armagnac.

diva**dos**

The fruit must be firm or it will cook to a mush. This recipe is also excellent with firm, sweet apricots, when, in season.

This can be cooked ahead of time, then gently reheated to serve.

Serve with crème fraîche, Greek yogurt or ice-cream and biscotti or your favorite cookies.

desserts and baking ingredients

Rich, creamy, and fragrant, that's what most dessert ingredients are all about. Core ingredients aside, they are responsible for the "oohs" and "aahs" when guests take that first mouthful! Quality and freshness are paramount, and please don't consider low-fat versions of dairy products – their flavor is inferior and they can alter a dessert's consistency.

CORE INGREDIENTS

Butter: We prefer salted butter for its creamy flavor, unless unsalted butter is specified. Butter freezes well or stores in the fridge for several weeks. Margarine should be avoided at all costs.

Flour: We recommend using Italian 00 flour for all our pastry recipes. You'll need white bread flour for breadmaking, ordinary all-purpose flour for sauces, and self-rising flour for cakes and scones.

Eggs: Eggs should be as fresh as possible and should be kept in the fridge. Remove and allow them to stand at room temperature for 10 minutes before using. When making meringues, it is imperative that the eggs are not cold, otherwise the whites will not whisk properly. We use medium-size eggs unless otherwise stated.

Sugar: Granulated is the most useful, especially if it is ground finer in a food processor. Soft brown sugar comes from unrefined cane sugar and provides good color and flavor. Sifted confectioner's sugar is excellent dusted over hot and cold desserts.

CREAMS, YOGURTS AND CREAM CHEESES

Heavy cream: Also called heavy whipping cream, has one of the highest fat contents – around between 36 and 40 percent. The higher the fat, the more sturdy it is when whipped. This rich, thick cream is used for cooking and whipping, and is excellent for roulades, meringues, and pouring over desserts. Mix with soft fruits, curds, melted chocolate, vanilla, or liqueurs for more flavor.

Light Cream: Also called coffee or table cream, contains between 18 to 30 percent fat, averaging around 20 percent. It is best used for topping hot desserts, adding to soups, hot drinks, or sauces.

Whipping Cream: Is similar to heavy cream but with a lower fat content of between 30 to 36 percent. When whisked, it produces a light, airy texture, ideal for cream-based desserts.

Sour Cream: This sour-flavored cream is similar to crème fraîche. A simple fruit tart can be made with a mixture of sour cream, sugar, eggs, orange zest, and fresh berries poured into a pie shell and baked for 30 minutes.

Crème Fraîche: Created by adding buttermilk, sour cream, or yogurt to cream. Crème fraîche is rich and creamy with a slight tang. It's superb served with fruit tarts and chocolate cakes. Because it's a cultured product, it doesn't curdle when boiled,

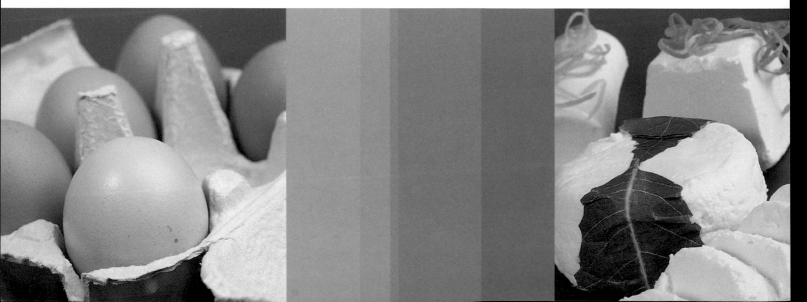

so it's a useful cooking cream. It keeps well in the fridge.

Greek Yogurt: This thick and creamy yogurt is one of our favorite ingredients. It has a great sharp flavor, which lends itself to desserts and is divine with fruit. Also wonderful with many savory dishes.

Mascarpone Cheese: The key ingredient of tiramisu, this delicious Italian cheese is made by curdling thick cream, and has a high fat content (around 47 percent). It has a sweetish flavor and can be used to replace cream. Serve with tarts, poached pears, or chocolate cakes. It also makes fantastic crème brûlée and ice-cream. Unfortunately, it isn't readily available at all supermarkets; your best bet is to check Italian delis or gourmet shops.

Mild goat cheese: A light, creamy cheese that's far milder than the drier, rinded variety and very versatile. We like the variety sold in small tubs, which keep well in the fridge. If goat cheese is unavailable, then cream cheese can be used as a substitute in many recipes.

Cream Cheese: Simply luscious for cheesecakes but excellent for a range of sweet dishes.

Fromage Frais: Although used in the same way as yogurt and cream, fromage frais is actually a cheese. It can replace yogurt but it doesn't heat well, so it is used mainly in cold dishes.

CHOCOLATE

White Chocolate: Contains no cocoa solids, so it has a pale appearance and a mild, sweet taste. It's good for cookies and useful for coating and decorating. It burns easily, so melt gently over simmering water.

Dark Chocolate: Figuring out what kind of chocolate to buy can be confusing, but we believe that price is generally a good indicator of quality. It should contain a high percentage of cocoa solids, the higher the better, and this figure is usually stated on the label. Top-quality European chocolate has around 75 percent cocoa solids and an intense flavor – ideal for rich desserts. Bittersweet, semisweet, or baking chocolates have less cocoa butter and therefore lower quality, but can still produce good desserts.

CITRUS FRUITS

Oranges, lemons, limes, and grapefruit are essential ingredients in dessert-making, and should be used both for flavoring and garnishing. Orange and pink grapefruit segments look stunning with mint for decorating a meringue or cake, grated zests are lovely in pastry, and citrus-fruit juices

are wonderful mixed with cream and eggs for a tart filling.

NUTS

Nuts are tasty for all cooking, but they are especially good for baking and desserts. We find almonds, hazelnuts, pistachio nuts, pine nuts, and walnuts the most useful. For an intense flavor, roast and grind your own: scatter the nuts on a baking sheet and place in a moderately hot oven for 8–10 minutes until golden. Cool, then grind in a food processor. Homemade praline with hazelnuts, pecans, or almonds is delicious and can be crushed and added to ice-cream.

VANILLA

Vanilla pods are the dried seed-cases of a tropical orchid and have a fragrant aroma. Although expensive, pods can be washed, dried, and re-used several times and blended with sugar. The pods are used mainly for flavoring creams and liquids, and then removed after infusing. For extra flavor, add the seeds: cut open the pod lengthwise and scrape out the seeds with a knife. Pure vanilla essence is created by extracting the flavor from the pods with alcohol. It is commonly used in cakes and cookies, and should be used sparingly, as it has a strong flavor. Vanilla extract is milder and more diluted, and, like essence, it is sold in a liquid form.

double chocolate mascarpone tart

● Serves: 8-10   ● Preparation: 30 minutes chiling and 20 minutes   ● Cooking: 50 minutes

What could be more decadent combination than a flaky chocolate crust and a creamy filling of mascarpone cheese and dark chocolate? A deliciously tempting dessert for serious chocoholics!

chocolate pastry

1¼ cups (5½ oz) all-purpose flour

1 tablespoon confectioner's sugar

2 tablespoons dark cocoa powder

7 tablespoons (3½ oz) salted butter, chilled

1 medium egg

filling

7 oz dark chocolate, broken into pieces

1 lb 5 oz mascarpone cheese

⅔ cup (5½ oz) sugar

3 medium eggs

1 tablespoon brandy

1 Preheat the oven to 350°F.

2 To make the pastry, place the flour, sugar, cocoa powder, and butter in a food processor and blend until the mixture resembles fine breadcrumbs. Add the egg and mix briefly to form a firm dough.

3 Roll out the pastry thinly on a lightly floured surface, then use it to line an 8-inch loose-bottomed, deep tart pan. Prick the base several times with a fork. Chill for 30 minutes.

4 Place a piece of non-stick baking parchment paper in the tart shell, fill with baking beans and bake for 10 minutes. Remove the beans and paper, and bake for another 5 minutes.

5 Remove the tart shell and reduce the oven temperature to 300°F.

6 For the filling, begin by melting the chocolate in a bowl over a pan of simmering water or in a microwave on medium power.

7 Beat the mascarpone cheese with the sugar and eggs. Divide the mixture between 2 bowls. Add the melted chocolate to one-half and the brandy to the other.

8 Spoon each mixture alternatively into the tart shell so that it will be layered all through. Bake at the same temperature for 35 minutes or until just set. Chill for 2 hours before serving.

diva**dos**

 If mascarpone cheese is not available, use cream cheese. Use good-quality, dark cocoa powder for the pastry.

Make the day before serving and keep covered in a cool place.

Don't worry if the filling takes a while to set. It's best cooked at a low oven temperature.

 Serve with fresh summer fruit, such as raspberries or strawberries.

pineapple tarte tatin with star anise

- Serves: 8   • Preparation: 20 minutes   • Cooking: 30-35 minutes

Tarte tatin can be made with almost any fruit. Our friend Julie, a brilliant dessert-maker, inspired us with this luscious combination of fresh pineapple, star anise, and caramel on flaky puff pastry.

7 oz puff pastry

about ½ cup (3 oz) sugar

3 tablespoons (1½ oz) unsalted butter

2 star anise, crushed in a spice mill

½ teaspoon ground cinnamon

1 vanilla pod, split and scraped

1 large fresh pineapple (weighing about 2 lb), peeled, cored, and sliced into ¼–inch pieces

1 Preheat the oven to 375°F. Roll out the pastry to a 10-inch round, so that it's slightly larger than an 8-inch pie pan (not loose-bottomed) or tarte tatin pan. (Alternatively, you can make 8 individual tarts in tart pans lined with non-stick baking parchment paper.)

2 To make the caramel, heat the sugar and butter together in a saucepan, stirring a little at first until the sugar has dissolved. Then cook, without stirring, until it forms a bubbling, golden caramel. Stir in the crushed star anise, cinnamon, and the vanilla seeds and pod. Pour the caramel into the tart pan.

3 Place the pineapple evenly over the base of the pan or divide evenly among the individual tart pans. Bake for 12 minutes.

4 Remove tart(s) from the oven and place the pastry on top, tucking the edges down the sides. Prick 6 times with a fork and bake for another 20 minutes, until the pastry is crisp and golden.

5 Cool for at least 5 minutes, then invert the tart(s) onto a plate. Remove the vanilla pod.

diva**dos**

Make the day before and reheat for 10–15 minutes in a moderately hot oven before serving.

Perfect little non-stick tarte tatin pans are available in good kitchen shops.

Serve warm as the grand finale to an Asian or Indian meal. It's delicious with either ice-cream or crème fraîche.

diva**don'ts**

Don't buy a ripe pineapple that is too soft, as it may have rotten spots in it.

fresh fig and plum tarte tatin with hot-fudge sauce

• Serves: 8   • Preparation: 25 minutes   • Cooking: 40 minutes

This dessert boasts stunning, dark-purple colors and autumn flavors. Delicious made individually or as a whole tart.

8 firm, dark plums, halved and pitted

4 tablespoons (2 oz) unsalted butter

½ cup (4 oz) sugar, plus
1 tablespoon extra

7 oz puff pastry

16 fresh figs, halved and cored

1 teaspoon ground cinnamon

fudge sauce

⅓ cup (2¾ oz) light soft brown sugar

4 tablespoons (2 oz) unsalted butter

3 tablespoons heavy (whipping) cream

1 Preheat the oven to 375°F.

2 Place the plums on a baking sheet, dot with 2 tablespoons (1 oz) of the butter and sprinkle with ¼ of the sugar. Bake for 20 minutes until soft.

3 Roll the pastry out thinly and cut out 8 x 4-inch circles with a large cookie cutter. Or, if making one large tart, use a large dinner plate for cutting around. Chill until needed.

4 Melt the remaining butter and the remaining measured amount of sugar together in a saucepan, stirring a little until the sugar has dissolved. Then cook, without stirring, until it forms a bubbling, golden caramel. Pour immediately into 8 individual tarte tatin pans, 8 ramekins or 1 large tart pan (not loose-bottomed).

5 Place the figs, cut side down, on top of the caramel, and press down firmly. Sprinkle with cinnamon and the extra 1 tablespoon sugar. Place 2 plums halves in each tart or arrange evenly in the large tart.

6 Top the tarts with the chilled pastry rounds, tucking the edges down the sides so as to create a rim when the tart(s) is inverted. Prick 6 times with a fork. Place on a large baking sheet and bake for 20 minutes, until crisp and golden.

7 Place all the ingredients for the sauce in a saucepan and bring to a boil, whisking to combine.

8 Invert the tart(s) onto warm plates and serve with the hot-fudge sauce.

diva**dos**

This recipe is best made in late summer or autumn, when figs are in season and plums are sweet but firm.

This tart is extra-delicious served with crème fraîche.

The tart(s) can be made the day before, then reheated for 15 minutes in a moderately hot oven. This works well, as the color improves and they become a little firmer, so are easier to turn out and serve.

chocolate and amaretti meringue roulade

● Serves: 8   ● Preparation: 15 minutes   ● Cooking: 15 minutes

This sounds quintessentially Christmassy, but is actually so versatile that you can serve it all year round. It tastes wonderful with summer berries and is a chocolate-lover's dream.

meringue

5 medium egg whites

a pinch of salt

1¼ cups (9 oz) sugar

3 tablespoons dark cocoa powder, sifted

filling

1⅛ cups (9 fl oz) heavy (whipping) cream

3 oz amaretti biscuits, crushed

3 tablespoons amaretto liqueur or brandy

1 Preheat the oven to 325°F. Line a 10 x 14-inch Swiss roll pan with non-stick baking parchment paper.

2 Whisk the egg whites with the salt until stiff, then gradually whisk in the sugar, a couple of tablespoons at a time. Fold in the cocoa powder. Spread the meringue mixture evenly in the pan.

3 Bake for 15 minutes until crispy on the outside. Remove from the oven and cool.

4 Whip the cream until stiff, then fold in the crushed cookies and liqueur or brandy.

5 Turn the meringue out onto another sheet of non-stick baking parchment paper and carefully peel away the lining paper. Spread the cream mixture over the meringue and roll up lengthwise. Chill until needed, then serve cut into slices.

diva**dos**

Chopped stem ginger can be used instead of the amaretti biscuits. Use 3 pieces, drained of syrup, and chop finely.

Follow the golden rules of whisking egg whites: use room-temperature egg whites and a clean bowl to whisk them in, otherwise they will not thicken properly. The meringue can be made the day before, but fill and roll the roulade on the day of serving the dessert.

The meringue should be crispy when removed from the oven. If it's not, do not cook further, otherwise it will not roll well. It will crisp as it cools down.

Serve with caramelized pears (follow the recipe for Glazed Winter Fruits on page 147) and decorate with cape gooseberries (physalis). In the summer, the roulade is excellent drizzled with melted white chocolate and decorated with fresh berries.

chez panisse chocolate cake

● Serves: 8   ● Preparation: 20 minutes   ● Cooking: 25-30 minutes

Over the past years at Books for Cooks, there has always been a quest to find the perfect chocolate cake. We must have tried at least 50 different recipes, but always came back to this one. The famous Chez Panisse restaurant, outside San Francisco, is the creator of this fabulous recipe. It is the richest, fudgiest chocolate cake you will ever have.

9 oz dark chocolate, broken into pieces

1 cup plus 2 tablespoons (9 oz) salted butter

6 medium eggs, separated

½ teaspoon cream of tartar

¾ cup (6 oz) sugar

¼ cup (2 oz) light soft brown sugar

½ cup (2 oz) ground almonds

3 tablespoons all-purpose flour, sifted

sifted confectioner's sugar and/or cocoa powder to decorate

1 Preheat the oven to 375°F. Grease the base of an 8–9-inch springform cake pan and line with non-stick baking parchment paper. Dust with a little flour.

2 Melt the chocolate and butter in a bowl over a pan of simmering water or in a microwave on medium power. Once melted, whisk together until smooth.

3 Whisk the egg whites and cream of tartar with an electric mixer until soft peaks form.

4 Whisk the egg yolks in a large mixing bowl with both the sugars until thick and pale. Pour in the chocolate mixture, and mix gently until smooth.

5 Add the almonds and flour to the chocolate mixture and mix again. Carefully fold in the egg whites.

6 Pour the batter into the prepared pan. Bake for 25–30 minutes, until the cake is set but slightly wobbly in the center. Cool in the pan.

7 To serve, run a knife around the edge and remove the cake from the tin. Peel off the paper and place on a cake platter. Dust with confectioner's sugar and/or cocoa powder.

diva**dos**

Buy a good-quality dark chocolate.

The cake can be made up to 3 days before the party. Use eggs at room temperature. Make sure that your mixer bowl is spotlessly clean, or the egg whites will not whisk properly.

Serve with crème fraîche, mascarpone cheese or homemade ice-cream. This cake is delectably rich, so keep portions small.

diva**don'ts**

Don't refrigerate the cake if making ahead. Simply place foil over the top and leave at room temperature.

heavenly chunky-chewy chocolate cookies

● Makes: 30   ● Preparation: 20 minutes   ● Cooking: 10 minutes

Why not just double the quantity now? You'll never have enough! The most difficult thing about preparing these cookies is trying not to eat them before they're ready to be served!

1 cup (4½ oz) all-purpose flour

3 level tablespoons (1 oz) dark cocoa powder

½ teaspoon baking soda

a pinch of salt

4½ oz dark chocolate, broken into pieces

6 tablespoons (3 oz) unsalted butter

⅔ cup (6 oz) soft brown sugar

2 small eggs

1 teaspoon pure vanilla extract

12 oz dark chocolate chips

2 oz white chocolate, broken into pieces

1 Preheat the oven to 350°F. Sift together the flour, cocoa powder, baking soda, and salt into a bowl.

2 Gently melt the dark chocolate in a bowl over a pan of simmering water or in a microwave on medium power.

3 Cream the butter and sugar together until light and fluffy, then beat in the eggs, vanilla, and melted chocolate.

4 Stir the chocolate chips and white chocolate pieces into the creamed mixture, mix well, then add the flour mixture. Stir well.

5 Line 3–4 large baking sheets with non-stick baking parchment paper and place 30 heaped tablespoons of the cookie mixture onto the tray. Bake for 10 minutes.

6 Cool slightly for several minutes, then remove with a spatula or palette knife and cool on a wire rack.

really good, but needs more liquid .

diva**dos**

 Dark chocolate chips are readily available, but white chocolate chunks are better than using white chocolate chips.

These are best made on the day of eating, but can be made several days before. Store in an airtight container. Reheat in a very low oven for just 5 minutes, if you like them slightly soft and chewy.

diva**don'ts**

Do not overcook – better to undercook, since they should be soft and chewy!

diva**breads**

diva breadsticks

- Makes: 25 breadsticks
- Preparation: 1 hour proving and 30 minutes
- cooking: 20 minutes

Try our basic Olive Oil and Sea Salt Bread (see page 160) twisted with the lusty fillings listed below. You can serve these breadsticks warm.

FILLINGS

garlic and rosemary confit

3 garlic bulbs, unpeeled

3 tablespoons olive oil

¼ cup (2 fl oz) balsamic vinegar

1 tablespoon chopped rosemary

½ teaspoon each salt and pepper

parmesan, red onion, and prosciutto

2 tablespoons olive oil

2 red onions, thickly sliced

½ teaspoon each of salt and pepper

25 thin slices of proscuitto, diced

1¾ oz Parmesan cheese, grated

olive, chili, and fennel seed

about ½ cup (3½ oz) pitted Italian black olives, chopped

2 tablespoons fennel seeds

1 teaspoon crushed dried red chilies

1 tablespoon each of salt and pepper

1 Preheat the oven to 400°F.

2 Follow the basic recipe for Olive Oil and Sea Salt Bread (page 160). After proving, when the dough has doubled in size, punch down and knead for 2 minutes, then roll out into a large square. Spread your chosen filling (see below) over one half and fold the dough over. Press down with your fingertips. Slice the dough into 25 long, thin slices. Roll each slice back and forth with the palms of your hands, then twist the ends.

3 Place the sticks on baking sheets covered with baking parchment, sprinkle with salt and pepper, and bake for 20 minutes, until golden brown. Then cool.

diva**dos**

 Use good-quality olives. Remove any excess fat from the prosciutto.

Prepare the breadstick fillings the day ahead, but try to bake the sticks fresh to serve.

garlic and rosemary confit

Blanch the garlic cloves for 3 minutes in boiling water. Drain and refresh under cold running water. Peel each clove. Heat the oil in a medium saucepan and lightly brown the garlic. Add the vinegar, rosemary, salt, pepper, and 4 tablespoons of water. Cook gently for 3 minutes, until the mixture is syrupy.

parmesan, red onion, and prosciutto

Heat the olive oil in a frying pan, add the onions, salt and pepper; fry until soft, then place in a bowl with the prosciutto and Parmesan cheese.

olive, chili, and fennel seed

Mix the ingredients together in a small bowl.

olive oil and sea salt bread

● Preparation: 1 hour proving and 10 minutes   ● Cooking: 20 minutes

We've always had a love-hate relationship with making bread. Sometimes it worked and other times it didn't! It wasn't until we went to the organic bakery in Penrith for a weekend that we sorted ourselves out. This is one of the most simple and foolproof of recipes for making bread. It doesn't require any sourdough starter or lengthy proving time. Use this master recipe for most of the breads in this chapter.

1 oz dried yeast

a pinch of sugar

1 pint (16 fl oz) tepid water

2 lb strong white (bread) flour, preferably organic

1 teaspoon sea salt

½ cup (4 fl oz) olive oil

1 Stir the yeast and sugar into the tepid water and leave for 5–10 minutes, until it starts to froth.

2 Combine the flour and salt in a large bowl, then add the olive oil and yeast liquid. Mix with a large wooden spoon or your hands to bring together into a soft, springy dough. Remove from the bowl and place on a lightly floured surface. Knead for 5 minutes until you have a smooth, elastic

dough. If the dough feels heavy and dry, add a drop more water to it and keep kneading.

3 Place the dough in a large, lightly oiled bowl and cover tightly with plastic wrap. Leave to rise in a draught-free place for 1 hour, or until doubled in size. Take the dough out and knead for a few minutes.

4 Follow individual recipes from here.

diva**dos**

One of the reasons bread can have a close texture is because the dough is lacking in moisture. The stiffness keeps it from rising properly, so add a little more water – but not too much, as this can make the bread heavy.

Having a warm environment for the dough to prove is ideal. If your house is cold and draughty, heat your oven to 250°F for 5 minutes. Turn off and place the covered bowl of bread inside. Leave to rise for the required time.

miniature focaccia topped with caramelized onions

● Makes: about 25 mini breads   ● Preparation: 20 minutes   ● Cooking: 45 minutes

Irresistible little flavored breads, which are ideal for parties.

1 quantity Olive Oil and Sea Salt Bread (see page 160)

topping

3 red onions, cut into wedges

4 tablespoons olive oil

2 tablespoons balsamic vinegar

1 tablespoon (½ oz) butter

sea salt and pepper

rosemary or thyme sprigs

1 Preheat the oven to 375°F. Place the onions in a roasting pan, drizzle with oil and vinegar, dot with butter, and season with salt and pepper. Roast for 30 minutes, shaking a couple of times during cooking.

2 Follow the basic method for the Olive Oil Bread (page 160), until it has proven and doubled in size.

3 Increase the oven temperature to 425°F. Turn the dough out on a lightly floured surface and divide into about 25 x 2-oz pieces. Briefly shape into rounds, then press each ball down with your fingertips. Place the mini focaccia on 2 lightly oiled baking sheets.

4 Top each bread with some of the caramelized onions and a herb sprig, then sprinkle with a little sea salt. Bake for 15 minutes, or until the bread sounds hollow when tapped underneath. Place on a wire rack to cool. Serve warm or at room temperature.

diva**dos**

Use good-quality strong plain (bread) flour for making the dough. Other strong-flavored herbs such as sage can be used and, if desired, try placing a small piece of blue cheese on the bread, pushing it into the dough under the onions.

Do cover the dough properly when rising, as draughts can inhibit the rising process. If more convenient, make the dough the night before and leave it in the fridge to rise overnight. Bring back to room temperature before shaping.

cumin flatbread

● Makes: 2 loaves ● Preparation: 1 hour proving and 15 minutes ● Cooking: 15 minutes

This spicy garlic bread has a brilliant yellow color and tasty bits of cumin in every bite.

1 lb 2 oz strong white (bread) flour

1 tablespoon salt

2 tablespoons cumin seeds, toasted and crushed

1 oz fresh yeast or ½ oz dried yeast

pinch of sugar

1⅛ cups (9 fl oz) tepid water

⅓ cup plus 1 tablespoon (3 fl oz) olive oil

2 garlic cloves, finely chopped

1 teaspoon turmeric

1 large handful fresh cilantro, chopped

1 Put the flour, salt, and toasted cumin seeds in a large bowl. Dissolve the yeast and sugar in the warm water and leave for 5 minutes, until frothy. Warm the olive oil in a small pan and add the garlic, turmeric, and cilantro. Leave the garlic to soften slightly for 5 minutes, then remove the pan from the heat. Leave to cool.

2 Add the cooled oil to the flour mixture, pour in the yeasted water, and mix into a smooth dough with your hands. Knead for about 5 minutes on a lightly floured work surface, until the dough is smooth, elastic, and no longer sticky.

3 Place the dough in a lightly oiled bowl, cover with plastic wrap or a dish towel and leave in a draught-free place for 1 hour, or until doubled in size.

4 Preheat the oven to 425°F.

5 Punch down the dough, knead again for a few minutes, then roll out on a lightly floured surface into 2 x 7-inch flat circles. Place on 2 greased baking sheets and allow to rest for 5 minutes.

6 Bake for 15 minutes, until the loaves sound hollow when tapped underneath. Cool on wire racks.

diva**dos**

 You can vary the herbs and spices used for this bread.

Make the dough a day ahead, then leave it to prove in the fridge overnight. Bring back to room temperature before continuing.

Do ensure that the oven is properly preheated.

Serve with Salad Mezze Plate, Spicy Shrimps with Moroccan Tomato Jam and Filo Tart with Charmoula Chicken (see pages 122, 27 and 52). You can make lots of little spiced flatbreads instead of 2 large ones. Bake for 15 minutes.

diva**cooking**

herbs and spices

What would the world be without herbs and spices? Pretty boring. Home-grown herbs fresh from your garden are invaluable, or visit markets to find large bunches. Dried spices go stale after six months, so check the shelf life.

SOUTHEAST ASIAN HERBS

Cilantro: This gorgeous herb lends itself to most highly seasoned food. The roots and stems are essential for curry pastes, while the leaves go into salads, curries, salsas, and sauces.

Galangal: Similar to its cousin ginger, galangal is prepared in the same way. It has a medicinal odor that works in curry pastes and coconut-milk soups.

Lemongrass: Prized for its lime-and-lemon flavor in Thai soups, salads, and curries. Use the lower (bottom) portion, which is the most tender part. Crush the stem with a knife and peel away the outer layers. Finely chop the remainder for oriental stocks or teas. Lemongrass freezes well.

Lime Leaves: These aromatic leaves from the Thai kaffir lime tree add a lemony flavor to soups, curries, and salads. Finely shred the leaves for salads; leave whole for other dishes. They freeze well, but lose their color.

Thai Sweet Basil: Related to Italian basil, the Thai variety looks similar but is more aromatic, adding a distinctive flavor to salads and soups. Keep basil wrapped in wet paper towels and chilled, as it goes off quickly.

MEDITERRANEAN and MIDDLE EASTERN HERBS

Basil: There is no other aroma like a whiff of pungent basil. It can transform tomatoes and salads, taking them to a whole new level.

Flat-leaf (Italian) Parsley: Almost considered a vegetable in the Middle East because it's so often used. Superior to the curly variety, it is crucial for Mediterranean salads, sauces, and meats. Use the stems for stock and in bouquet garni.

Mint: There are more than 200 varieties, but spearmint has the best taste. It's great in salads, marinades, and herb sauces as well as cool drinks.

Oregano: This herb pairs well with tomatoes, poultry, and meats. Use sparingly – the flavor is powerful.

Rosemary: Excellent with meats, fish, poultry, and beans. Needles should be finely chopped. The stems can be used for barbecue skewers (see page 20).

Sage. An Italian favorite, it's delicious deep-fried on ravioli, pasta, risotto, poultry, or game dishes, and is key for stuffings and roasts.

Tarragon: An assertive French herb, classically used for béarnaise sauce and remoulade mayonnaise. Delicious with poultry, fish, and cold meats and makes a dreamy partner for tomatoes.

DRIED SPICES

ITALIAN

Fennel Seed: With its sweet liquorice flavor, whole fennel seed complements salads, vegetables, roasts, and breads. When crushed, it can add a subtle taste to risottos or pastas.

Saffron: An expensive spice, thankfully used in small amounts! We prefer saffron threads – they hold their flavor longer. Powdered saffron can be deceptive since it's often adulterated. To draw out more flavor and color, infuse saffron in 2 tablespoons of boiling water before using.

CHINESE

Five Spice: A pungent, dry spice-mix made from cinnamon, cloves, fennel, star anise, and Szechuan peppercorns. It's excellent with roast pork and duck and wonderful when sprinkled on Asian roast vegetables.

Star Anise: Used mostly with poultry, game, and fruit desserts, this spice infuses an exotic liquorice taste. Leave whole or grind finely in a spice mill.

INDIAN AND ASIAN SPICES

Cardamom: A spicy-sweet aromatic that adds flavor to stews, curries and chutneys, but also works well used subtly in cream. Crush in a mortar and pestle, discarding the pods to leave the seeds.

Cinnamon: This sweet, fragrant spice enhances all desserts, tagines, and stews. Grind your own sticks for the freshest flavor and use whole sticks to infuse mulled wines and fruit punches.

Coriander Seeds: Popular since ancient times, coriander's spicy taste complements meats and vegetables. Toasting and grinding the seeds is almost effortless and makes a big flavor difference.

Cumin: A popular and extremely versatile spice. The nutty, peppery seeds can be ground with other spices for curries, or used whole with vegetables and meats.

Ground Ginger: Very different to fresh, and used mostly in Indian curries and North African tagines.

It's a key flavoring in curry spice mixtures and also works well in tarts, cakes, and hot desserts.

Turmeric: Widely used in curries and tagines, turmeric provides a powerful flavor and brilliant color. Terrific with root vegetables such as potatoes, or for brightening up rice – just add to the cooking water.

LATIN AMERICAN AND OTHER GROUND CHILI SPICES

Chili Powder: The key flavor in beef or black-bean chili, this is made from ground dried chilies. Great for grilled meats or vegetables in tortilla wraps.

Crushed Red Chilies: When that extra kick is needed, this is the all-purpose spice to do the job. Pasta, seafood, and chicken as well as salads taste perfect with a little heat added.

Ground Cayenne Pepper: For more subtle heat, add cayenne by the pinch. It's especially good when added to potato or crab cakes.

Paprika: The Hungarian variety is considered to be the best and varies from mild and sweet to hot. Our favorite is the Spanish *pimentón*, which has a smoky aroma. It complements seafood, sauces, salsas, meats, stews, and rice dishes.

strong ethnic flavors

Go to any ethnic supermarket and you'll find a treasure-trove of exotic ingredients. If you live in a remote area, remember that many shops have a mail-order service, or browse the internet to find specialty stores and buy more unusual items online.

ITALIAN

Capers: Add a piquant, salty flavor to any dish. Those packed in salt are superior to brined, but soak them before using. Teamed with their soul-mate, anchovies, capers have a magical depth. Excellent in fish or poultry dishes.

Caperberries: Popular as an antipasti component or baked with poultry, caperberries could soon replace olives as your favorite snack. They are left on the caper shrub longer than capers, producing a seedy texture.

Olives: For recipes, look for the black variety mixed with olive oil and herbs – they are mild in flavor and won't overpower the dish. Please don't use canned. Fortunately it is now possible to buy good-quality, pitted olives.

Dried Mushrooms: Italian porcini and French ceps add a huge flavor dimension to meat and poultry dishes. Soak for 20 minutes in boiling water and use the soaking liquid as stock.

Rinse well before using, because they can be quite sandy.

Saba: A new ingredient to come on the market, though it dates back to Roman times. It is prepared from concentrated grape musk and is fantastic in sauces for game and poultry, and in salad dressings.

CHINESE

Hoisin Sauce: Made from soya beans, garlic, and chilies, this sweet and spicy sauce is a boost for Asian marinades and sauces.

Soy Sauce: This dark, salty sauce complements any Asian dish. We prefer the light Japanese soy sauce to the dark, which can be too heavy and salty.

Sweet Chili Bean Paste: Gorgeous stuff made from fermented soya beans or black beans, chilies, and garlic. It is essential for peanut dipping sauces and noodle dishes.

JAPANESE

Saké: Made from rice, saké is not only Japan's favorite alcohol, it's also used in cooking for sauces and marinades, and for toning down strong flavors.

Mirin: A milder, thicker version of saké, mirin adds a lovely sweetness to Asian sauces, dressings, marinades and glazes. It's particularly great in dressings for noodle salads, chicken, or fish.

Miso Paste: The peanut butter of Japan, miso is made from fermented soya beans. There are 3 varieties available: yellow, red, and brown. Use the lighter colors for soups and sauces, and the dark for heavy dishes. Miso is excellent in Asian marinades, vinaigrettes and glazes.

THAI

Fish Sauce (Nam Pla): This is used in just about everything in Southeast Asia. Made of fermented anchovies,

this essential sauce imparts a salty, pungent and sharp taste to dressings, sauces and curries. When paired with lime juice, sugar, and chilies, it's pure magic.

Sweet Chili Dipping Sauce: This syrupy condiment made of chili, garlic, sugar, and rice-wine vinegar is the perfect dipping sauce – delicious with fried foods, Thai salads, or mixed with coconut milk for sauces. It is honestly better in a bottle than making your own!

Tom Yum Paste: Made of chilies, galangal (like ginger), lemongrass, and lime leaves. We love this spicy, hot and sour-tasting paste in Asian curries, soups, and sauces.

KOREAN

Kochujang: A sweet and spicy chili paste that's superb in marinades for beef, poultry, or seafood. Best found in Japanese or Korean food stores.

Sesame Oil: Fantastic for its nutty, smoky flavor, and great for marinades, dressings, and stir-fries. Do not keep for too long or it will lose its beautiful fragrance.

INDONESIAN

Ketchap Manis: This dark, seductive soy sauce is thicker and sweeter than its Chinese cousin. Use as a condiment for canapés, stir-fry with noodles, and add to sauces and salsas.

Sambal Oelek: A concentrated mixture of chilies, brown sugar, and salt. It makes a brilliant shortcut for any recipe using chopped fresh chili. Remember that a little goes a long way.

MIDDLE EASTERN

Pomegranate Molasses: A Persian syrup made from reduced pomegranate juice. It has a sharp, sweet-and-sour flavor that makes an excellent marinade or glaze for lamb, duck, or chicken. It is also delicious used in dressings for couscous, vegetable salads, and grilled eggplant.

INDIAN

Tamarind: A major ingredient in Worcestershire sauce, this sweet-and-sour ingredient is a key flavor for Indian, Thai, and Mexican cooking. Buy tamarind as blocks of pulp, which are soaked in hot water and then sieved, or use bottled tamarind sold in supermarkets. We adore it in marinades, dips, and dressings.

MEXICAN

Ancho Chilies: Sweet, fruit-flavored chilies that are mild on the heat scale. They are sold dried and must be reconstituted in boiling water. They lend a beautiful taste to sauces for meats, marinades, and salsas.

Chipotles in Adobo Sauce: These little cans of smoky chilies packed in a garlicky tomato sauce are a must for every kitchen. A powerhouse of hot flavor, the chipotle is actually a dried and smoked jalapeño chili. Use carefully in dressings, marinades, potato salads, and sauces.

NORTH AFRICAN

Preserved Lemons: These make a lovely addition to tagines, salsas, salads, and marinades, adding a mysterious sweet-and-sour flavor. Make your own by cutting 5 lemons into quarters, placing in a sealed, sterilized jar with $2^3/_4$ oz of sea salt. Cover with lemon juice and leave for 2 weeks. To use, rinse and scoop away the flesh. Chop the skin finely .

Harissa Paste: A powerful wallop of flavor and heat sold in a tiny jar. Made of roasted chili peppers, cilantro, garlic, and olive oil, harissa is fantastic for tagines, couscous, salads, yogurt sauces, salsas, and marinades.

diva**parties**

Preparation is fundamental to making sure you and your guests enjoy your party. If you find yourself worrying about quantities or last-minute disasters, you will not have a good time, but with careful forward-planning you can relax as much as your guests. For the diva cook, sourcing the best ingredients, the freshest meat, the crispest salads, and the tastiest vegetables is all part of the fun. Follow our guidelines for menu-planning, quantities, shopping, preparation, and storage, and you can't fail to have a successful party.

planning

designing your menu

Good menu design ensures the cook never has too much to do and that a variety of guests are catered for.

- Consider your guests' tastes as well as any special dietary requirements.
- Give the party a theme that's easy to design around.
- Plan according to seasonal availability of ingredients.
- Know your budget. If you splurge on a main course, for instance, you may want to economize on others.
- Choose a menu that's convenient to prepare in the time available. Keep in mind the space you have and equipment you'll need.
- Balance colors, textures, and flavors throughout the meal.
- Serving three full courses is no longer *de rigueur*. Try offering a few canapés as a appetizer and replacing dessert with fruit and cheese – a good choice for a mid-week party.
- Rely on the party menu suggestions that follow this section – they offer tried-and-tested themes and a delicious balance of flavors.

knowing your quantities

Preparing too little food can be a disaster, while piles of uneaten dishes can take the shine off what was otherwise a huge success of a party. Following these tips should make sure your guests are well-fed and that you've used your party budget wisely.

canapés

- Pre-lunch canapés: 3–4 different canapés; allow 3–4 per head.
- Canapés served as a appetizer: 4 different canapés; allow 5 per head.
- Evening canapé party: 6–8 different canapés; allow 10 per head.
- Canapés served instead of a meal: 8 different canapés; allow 16 per head.

other dishes

- Guests will consume less food when standing than they do when sitting down, so adjust accordingly.

- When ordering prime cuts of meat or fish which have no bones or fat, we allow 4 servings to 1 pound. This is particularly accurate when using fillet of lamb or beef.
- Don't be tempted to serve too many different dishes, or the unique flavors of each recipe will just merge into one. We feel a spectacular main-course dish works well with no more than two side dishes.
- If you are serving canapés or an appetizer before the main course, don't serve too much – choose a few stunning canapés to take the edge off people's hunger – not fill them up!

shopping

Shopping is all about getting fantastic, really fresh, and exotic ingredients in the right quantities – and with the minimum amount of fuss. Today, buying wonderful food for parties is easier than ever, especially if you follow our guidelines.

- Place your order for meat, fish, and other specialty ingredients 1 week ahead of the event in order to avoid disappointment.
- Try to purchase from local suppliers. The quality is normally high and they often deliver.
- Supermarkets may make home deliveries if you shop via the internet. This is worthwhile when ordering heavy dry goods, drinks, and household products. We don't, however, recommend that you allow a supermarket to choose your meats, vegetables, or other fresh goods. To ensure the best quality, do this in person.
- Organic foods are now widely available and are sometimes, though not always, superior. Be choosy about what you buy to make sure that the product is worth the price. Organic meat and poultry are sure bets for taste, but the quality of vegetables may be inconsistent.
- Think quality, quality, and quality again when choosing your meats and produce. But remember: the most expensive doesn't always equate to the best quality. Farmers' markets are ideal places for finding superb foods at reasonable prices.
- To avoid repeated, frustrating searches for unusual ethnic ingredients, find a good source, buy large quantities, and store your purchases. If you live far from a metropolitan area, consider ordering these ingredients online and having them sent directly to your home. This can be a godsend!
- Visiting local ethnic grocers is a marvellous adventure. Whether the shop is Greek, Chinese, Thai, Indian, or some other nationality, there's a fascinating new world to discover. You will appreciate the outstanding variety and quality, and you'll learn a thing or two about another culture's cuisine.
- Attempt to shop seasonally, as this affects flavor and prices enormously.
- Buy meat up to 2 days in advance.
- Because fish should be as fresh as possible when eaten, pre order all fish and seafood and collect on the day you plan to cook.
- Obtain salad, herbs, and soft fruits no more than 1 day ahead of your party.
- Purchase winter salad, such as chicory and spinach, 1–2 days before you prepare it.

storage

Once you get your shopping home, it is crucial to store all of the ingredients carefully in order to avoid spoilage.

vegetables and fruit

lettuces Keep in a dark, cool place: a larder or fridge. If refrigerated, place in a large plastic bag and spray with a little water.

root vegetables Store in a dark, cool area for up to 1 week. Remove all plastic wrapping.

onions, shallots, and garlic Store in a basket in a dark, cool place for up to 2 weeks. Always remove plastic wrapping or sprouting will begin.

tomatoes Store in a basket at room temperature. Never refrigerate.

herbs Wash and place in a glass of water in the refrigerator. Most will only keep for up to 2 days, with the exception of parsley, which lasts for up to 5 days.

summer fruits Keep cool and dry for 2 days.

hard fruits Store these in a dark, cool area for up to 1 week.

meat, poultry, and fish

meat Chill on a plate, uncovered, for up to 2 days.

fish Chill, loosely covered, for 1-2 days.

poultry Chill, covered for 1-2 days.

dairy

creams Store chilled, loosely covered.

eggs and butter Keep in a cool larder or fridge.

spices, nuts, oils, and pastes

dry spices Keep in a dry cool place for up to 6 months. Keep dried chilies in a refrigerator in order to prevent brittleness.

oils Store all oils for up to 6 months in a cool, dark cupboard. Walnut oil should be refrigerated and used quickly to ensure fragrance.

nuts Store in a dry, cool space or refrigerate. Use within 6 months to maintain freshness.

pastes Refrigerate all opened chili pastes and keep unopened in a dry, cool place.

equipment

Though you don't need to purchase every cooking gadget on the market, we hope our recommended list might help as a guide. Many of the items that appear on this list are essential for specific recipes in this book, but others aren't – they will simply make your life a little easier!

large electric food processor Buy one that does not have so many parts that it's impossible to clean.

sharp citrus-fruit squeezer

frying pan A heavy non-stick pan is versatile and long-lasting

knives We recommend that your collection includes 1 large heavy chopping knife, 1 small serrated knife, and 1 long carving knife. Purchase the best quality that you can afford and be sure to sharpen your knife blades regularly.

vegetable peeler There are many styles; use what feels most comfortable to you.

sharp cheese and citrus-fruit grater and zester Try to find a grater that grates finely, but is a normal shape.

food scales with ounces For absolutely accurate measurements.

large chopping boards Keep separate boards for meat and vegetables.

cake pans Removable-base springform pans, 8–9 inches wide.

tart pans Choose fluted, loose-bottomed 8–inch pans.

a cake mixer This lasts a lifetime and is particularly good for whisking egg whites very stiff.

roasting pans Large, high-quality pans will last longer.

individual 4–in cake pans Useful for making tarte tatins, both savory and sweet.

electric hand whisk Use it to whisk egg whites and whipping cream.

electric deep-fat fryer Choose a well-known brand that is easy to refill and clean.

large fine sieve Transferring ingredients into a tiny sieve can be a nightmare, so choose a good-sized one.

a large colander Small sizes are not as useful. Large

colanders are ideal for drip-drying washed salad leaves and efficiently draining vegetables and pasta.

a salad spinner There is no better way to thoroughly dry salad leaves so as not to dilute the dressing. Otherwise use a large, clean and dry dish towel to carefully shake the lettuce leaves dry.

mini-muffin pans A non-stick 12-muffin capacity pan is essential for making wonton cups and filo tartlets.

pastry brush Since they often lose bristles, either purchase a brush of superior quality or be prepared to buy many of cheaper construction.

cookie cutters Plain-edged cutters are probably the most useful. It makes good sense to buy a variety of sizes.

preparation and cooking schedule

Endless lists of ingredients to be bought and dishes to be prepared may seem daunting, but with simple planning, even apparently complex menus can be disarmingly straightforward.

1 week ahead

• Choose your menu and write out your shopping lists.

• Pre-order any important ingredients, such as meat, fish, fresh herbs.

• Write out a cooking preparation timetable for your party.

• If you are serving recipes that include pastry, you can make the pastry, line the pastry case, and freeze it uncooked.

• You can make crostini, filo tartlets, and other cases, and store in an airtight, dry container.

• Breads can be made, frozen, and then reheated when you are ready to serve them.

2 days ahead

• Do your party shopping.

• Make any vinaigrettes or dressings and keep covered in a cool place.

• Slow, braised meat dishes or soups are far better made several days in advance. Cover and store in the fridge.

• Both pestos and tapenades can be prepared ahead and then kept in an airtight container in a cool place.

• Mashed vegetables and purées can be prepared, chilled and reheated to serve.

• Our potato cake recipes work brilliantly made ahead and chilled. Fry to serve.

• Rice and couscous dishes can also be prepared ahead as long as you ensure that you cover well, chill, and reheat thoroughly when serving.

1 day ahead

• Fresh herbs and salads can be washed, dried well, and chilled in large, airy, plastic bags.

• Pick up any last-minute ingredients such as cheeses, breads, fruits, and fish.

• Marinate your meat, cover and chill, making sure that you turn the meat over in the marinade several times during the marinating time.

- Prepare vegetables and chill – be sure to keep root vegetables in cold water.
- Salsas and sauces that are appropriate can be made – leave out the fresh herbs until ready to serve.
- Make your dessert, as most can be made successfully a day ahead.
- Finish off baking any tarts that can be served cold or reheated.
- Vegetables can be blanched in salted water, drained and submerged into ice-water. Dry on paper towels, wrap, and refrigerate.

a few hours ahead

- Assemble cold canapés and leave garnishing until last.
- Decorate any cold desserts and leave in a cool place, but do not add such things as mint leaves until last, since they will absorb the mint flavor almost immediately.
- Fish can be seared several hours ahead. Simply brown it, chill immediately, and roast it just before serving.
- Sear the meat several hours ahead, ready to roast.
- Complete roasting the meat about 15 minutes before the meal, then allow it to rest for 10–15 minutes. Carve only to serve.
- Roast or blanch vegetables. Keep them warm or reheat to serve.
- Deep-fry any fried foods, drain on paper towels and keep warm in a medium to low oven to serve.
- Garnish foods with herbs just as you serve them to avoid them wilting.
- Assemble salads as late as possible to keep them fresh and light in appearance.

menu ideas

Planning exactly what dishes you want to match to create a party menu can be time-consuming and exhausting with so many fabulous diva dishes to choose from! So here's a list of a few of our favorites – we're sure they'll work as wonderfully for you as they have for us!

prepare-ahead party menu

Golden shallot pancakes with garlic and green olive tapenade
Goat cheese baked in spicy tomato sauce with garlic crostini
Gingered beef with honey and prunes
Pineapple tarte tatin with star anise

last-minute party food for fast lives

Tomato bruschetta with asparagus, gorgonzola, and basil salad
Seared tuna steaks with couscous and Sicilian vinaigrette
Chez Panisse chocolate cake

a taste of the orient

Vietnamese grilled pork in lettuce parcels
Thai green papaya salad with seared chili shrimp
Seared Thai chicken with tomato-chili jam
Fresh fig and plum tarte tatin with hot fudge sauce

mexican fiesta

Spiced corn cakes with avocado-lime salsa
Tuna ceviche on corn tortillas with mango salsa
Smoky chipotle chicken with pineapple salsa
Smoky black-bean tacos with cherry tomato salsa
Cinnamon pavlovas with carmelized apples and blackberries

summer sizzlers

Sun-blush tomato pesto with pita breadsticks
Avocado and goat cheese crostini with roasted cherry tomatoes

Grilled Mediterranean chicken salad with roasted garlic and basil dressing
Heavenly chunky-chewy chocolate cookies

winter warmer

Smoked trout on toasted bread with parsley and caper salsa
Caramelized red onion and fennel tarte tatin with olives and thyme
Monkfish, bacon, and dill pie with mashed potato, green green onions and parmesan
Cinnamon pavlova with caramelized apples and blackberries

an extravagant affair

Filo tarts of smoked salmon, tomato, and dill, with cucumber-lime salsa
Fennel and seafood bouillabaisse with saffron aïoli
Seared duck breasts with balsamic, rosemary, and shallot sauce
mashed sweet potatoes and ginger
Honey and mascarpone crème brûlée

a perfectly portable picnic

Sun-blush tomato pesto with pita breadsticks
Spicy grilled shrimp skewers with Moroccan tomato jam
Parsley and roasted garlic tart
Greek chicken salad with caper and anchovy vinaigrette
Fennel slaw with dill and cider dressing
Miniature foccacia topped with caramelized onions
Heavenly chunky chewy chocolate cookies

a party menu that freezes

Smoked fish tart with crème fraîche, lemon, and Parmesan
Balsamic chicken with porcini mushrooms
Chez Panisse chocolate cake

alfresco BBQ menu

Grilled shrimp with tamarind recado and avocado-red onion relish
Lamb fillet with roasted garlic, coriander and yogurt sauce
Tuscan panzanella salad
Babaganoush salad with goat cheese and crispy pita bread
New York cheesecake with fresh blueberries

formal dinner for 8

Asian salmon on star toast with chili crème fraîche
Marinated fig, glazed shallot, and prosciutto with Parmesan chips
mojo-marinated steaks with cilantro sauce and chilean salsa
Baby green salad with beet, green onion, and sesame
Caramelized new potatoes with tomato and soy
Chocolate and amaretti meringue roulade

canapés for a crowd

Filo tartlets with seared duck and tomato-sesame chutney
Mini Caesar salads en croute
Spiced corn cakes with avocado-lime salsa
Sri Lankan fishcakes with tomato sambal
Warm Gorgonzola wontons
Gingered chicken cakes with cilantro sauce

keep it hot: spicy party food

Crispy crab and cheese wontons with sweet chili dip
Asian salmon on star toast with chili crème fraîche
Shrimp, mint, and ginger spring rolls
Thai beef salad
Asian potato cakes with chili sambal
Korean chicken with cucumber salad
Sweet goat cheese, orange, and almond tart

think thai

Shrimp dumplings in fragrant Thai broth
Spicy crabcakes with cherry tomato and cilantro salsa
Seared Thai chicken with tomato-chili jam
Caramelized new potatoes with tomato and soy sauce
Pineapple tarte tatin with star anise

terrific pacific

Cucumber cups with Thai shrimp
Grilled Indonesian coconut chicken
Tamarind-roasted vegetables
Fresh fig and plum tarte tatin with hot-fudge sauce

tuscan nights

Tuscan panzanella salad
Spiedini of scallops with a chunky salsa verde
Slow-roasted Tuscan pork with fennel

Celeriac and roasted garlic purée
Glazed winter fruits with almond biscotti and crème fraîche

elegant evening
Filo tarts of smoked salmon, tomato, and dill with
cucumber-lime salsa
Gingered chicken cakes with cilantro sauce
Braised duck legs with soy, ginger, and star anise
Carmelized new potatoes with tomato and soy sauce
Honey and mascarpone crème brûlée

in praise of the tomato:
a late-summer menu
Roasted tomato and shallot tarte tatin
Butterflied leg of lamb with slow-roasted tomato, basil,
and olive confit
Saffron-roasted potatoes with rosemary and red onions
Pistachio and berry meringue roulade

a japanese influenced menu
Cucumber cups with Thai shrimp
Grilled teriyaki fillet of beef with noodles and soy dip
Miso-glazed cod
Chez Panisse chocolate cake

indelibly indian
Vegetable pakoras with cilantro and mint dip
Filo tartlets of seared duck with tomato-sesame chutney
Seared scallops and monkfish on curried red lentils with
yogurt sauce
Cinnamon pavlovas with caramalized apples and blackberries

very vegetarian menu
Polenta crusted eggplant with roasted tomatoes, buffalo
mozzarella, and salsa verde dressing
Wild mushroom and smoked mozzarella tart
Baby leaf salad with beets, green onion, and sesame
Chocolate and amaretti meringue roulade

middle eastern magic
Babaganoush salad with goat cheese and crispy pita bread
Mezze salad plate
Spiced cumin flatbread
Pomegranate-marinated lamb cutlets with coriander
tabbouleh
Pistachio and berry meringue roulade

gaucho grill

Spiced chicken empanaditas with green chili sauce

Mojo-marinated steak with cilantro sauce and Chilean salsa

Sweet goat cheese, orange, and almond tart

moroccan mystique

Spicy grilled shrimp skewers with Moroccan tomato jam

Filo tart with chermoula chicken

Moroccan carrots

Cinnamon pavlovas with caramelized apples and blackberries

veggies do lunch

Marinated fig, glazed shallot, and proscuitto salad
with Parmesan chips (omit the proscuitto)

Roasted tomato and shallot tarte tatin

Winter squash, roasted garlic, and gorgonzola galette

Diva breadsticks

Heavenly chunky-chewy chocolate cookies

pure mediterranean extravaganza

Golden shallot pancakes with garlic and green-olive tapenade

Spinach salad with crispy pancetta and warm
garlic dressing

Grilled red pepper stuffed with herbed ricotta and black
olive vinaigrette

Spiedini of scallops with a chunky salsa verde

Double chocolate mascarpone tart

indian vegetarian feast

Indian pakoras with two dips

Roasted winter vegetables in a fragrant coconut sauce

Coconut rice

Cumin flatbread

Pistachio and berry meringue roulade

quick and elegant

Warm Roquefort wontons

Grilled swordfish with rosemary, tomato, and
carmelized onions

Baby green salad with classic vinaigrette

Chez Panisse chocolate cake

veggies go to the middle east

Mezze salad plate

Babaganoush salad with goat cheese and crispy pita bread

Moroccan carrots

Couscous with roasted sweet potatoes and harissa dressing

Sweet goat cheese, orange, and almond tart

elegant autumn dinner

Mini Caesar salad en croute

Gratin of balsamic wild mushrooms

Butterflied leg of lamb with slow-roasted tomato, basil and
olive confit

Saffron roasted potatoes with rosemary and red onions

Glazed winter fruits

cool and refreshing for summer

Cucumber cups with Thai shrimp

Vietnamese chopped chicken salad

Grilled shrimp with Tamarind recado and pineapple and red
onion salsa

Soba noodle salad with shredded eggplant and soy-balsamic
dressing

New York cheesecake with fresh blueberries

brunch for a bunch

Grilled Mediterranean chicken salad with roasted garlic
and basil dressing

Tuscan panzanella salad

Broccoli, Italian sausage, and pecorino tart with roasted
cherry tomatoes

Filo tartlets of smoked salmon, tomato, and dill with
cucumber-lime salsa

Pistachio and berry meringue roulade

index